ANOT.
BRUMMIE IN BURMA

ISBN N° 1 903172 04 7

Published by Barny Books
Hough on the Hill, Grantham, Lincolnshire

Produced by: **TUCANN***design&print*, 19 High Street, Heighington, Lincoln LN4 1RG
Telephone and Fax: 01522 790009

CHAPTER ONE

W e lived in the Town as we used to call it, Friston Street, Ladywood; right near the city centre. Six of us lived there; Mom, Dad, sisters Irene, Laura and Vera and myself. Our house was typical of the time, a back to back type. The front door came off the street at the top of two stone steps. Everyday you would see the women scrubbing their steps, coating them with bath brick. On the ground floor was a small living room with the kitchen, or scullery as we called it, annexed off. Upstairs was the one main bedroom, with an attic bedroom above. There were no luxury fitted kitchens then, just a small black, old-fashioned gas stove and a small stone sink with a cold water tap. You had to heat the water yourself on the fire. It was a dangerous area because it was right next to the cellar steps. There was no protection, just an opening onto a very steep brick staircase. We all came a cropper at one time or another down those stairs. We had a door fitted in the end. That helped, but it was still dangerous, especially when going down to put money in the gas meter. It was a 'penny in the slot' type down there. Every Friday Mom would leave fourteen pennies on the top. This would usually last the week. We didn't have electricity, only gas and this was used for everything, including lighting. A candle or oil lamp had to be used for the cellar and attic. The gas pipe was in the middle of the ceiling with a regulator and mantle light fitting. It was a delicate operation to get it to work and if it was not adjusted properly it wouldn't work at all. There was no central heating either, just open coal fires. We only had these in the living room and main bedroom. There always seemed to be a fire going in the living room, but we only used the one in bedroom when it was really cold. The coal fires were rather hit and miss. If the wind blew the wrong way, the room would fill with thick black smoke, belched from the chimney. But they were very welcome in the cold weather and we would stand in front for a warm. The summer brought its own problems, the uninsulated attic was like a sauna, making sleep impossible and fleas and bed bugs flourished in the warm conditions. Everybody had them round us; it was a fact of life - there was no shame about it. We used 'Keatings' to get rid of them, plus physical extermination - a thumb or big finger. The latter method however, was frowned upon, as it made a mess of the wallpaper. We would clear them eventually and those that escaped would be killed off during the following winter as the cycle of our living conditions came round again.

The back door led out onto the entry, which in turn led to a rear communal yard, containing brick built brew or wash house and toilets, beyond which was four little back gardens, each about ten feet square. Some people built lean-to sheds to put their bikes in. We kept a few chickens on ours for some fresh eggs and for a fowl at Christmas. Dad tried to breed some once. He kept them in an old felt hat by the fire just after they hatched and put them outside when the weather got warmer. It was all right until they escaped. They got everywhere and a posse of neighbours was enlisted to round them up.

The wash house contained a large stone sink with cold water tap and a coal fired, copper boiler to heat the water. The women would take turns doing the family wash using a 'dolly', a wooden or copper cone with holes in, at the end of a long handle, used to thump the washing about to get the dirt out. Mom would cut up a chunk of sunlight soap to help and a 'blue bag' was used to get the whites really white. You would always see someone dollying their washing in one of the large wooden tubs outside the wash house. It was hard work. All the toilets were outside. We had to share them with other families in the block; usually two toilets between four families, about eighteen people. I didn't know anybody with an inside loo, only the posh people in Edgbaston had those. Ours were right at the top of the yard. The toilets themselves consisted of a long wooden board with two holes cut out with a thin timber-dividing panel between them. Families took turns to keep the toilets clean and change the toilet paper, small squares of newspaper threaded onto a nail on the back of the door. The door opened inwards which was quite fortunate as there was no lock, but you needed long legs, or a loud cough, to save embarrassment. Some people made it a bit of a social event, reading the paper, smoking a fag or having a chat, but most did what they had to do and got out.

The only break in the pattern of houses down the street was some small shops and general stores. Mrs Castle ran the general store. She sold everything there, from a loaf of bread to a gas mantle or a pair of shoelaces. Mom used to take us up the town on Saturdays. The Bull Ring was the place to go. The shops stayed open until all the perishable goods were sold. As it got later the prices came down. We stayed fairly late until what Mom wanted came into her price range, hopefully before it came into somebody else's. As we walked down Broad Street on the way home, we would call into 'Houghtons', the butchers, to see if we could pick up a cheap joint for the weekend. She would always buy us a penny plate of cockles in vinegar and have two fresh oysters herself. We shopped locally generally, with most things bought on 'tick', which was paid off every week. It was essential that the slate was cleared on Friday, payday, before any more credit was given and Mom and the shopkeeper would carefully check off every item.

Pubs were everywhere. The men would retreat to the Gents Only room for a few beers, a smoke of their Woodbines, or to read the Dispatch, the local paper. This was a very important pastime for the men in those days. Mom and Dad weren't heavy drinkers but they liked a glass of beer now and again. They would often send me to the outdoor with a jug to get three halves of ale. It cost sixpence and I would rush back home with it, perhaps taking a swig on the way providing Mom wasn't watching from the step. Betting was illegal then. The police would raid and fine the local bookie once a month to keep things under control. Dad liked a bet now and then, nothing big. From time to time, I would take Dad's bet down to the bookie. It was usually sixpence or a shilling wrapped in a bit of paper with the horse's names on it, signed with a fictitious name. I would take this down to the bookie's house, next to the coal merchant. A brick was missing next to the gate and the bet would be posted through the hole. A hand would be there to take it. Sometimes Dad would win, but usually he lost and Mom would moan about the waste of money.

From the age of five we all went to school and we stayed there until we were fourteen. There were no such things as nurseries. Very few women went out to work. It was the menfolk who had to earn the money and many were low paid or out of work. We didn't have school dinners. We came home for dinner at 12 o'clock. Mom had to shop and cook everyday. Money was tight so the food we had was basic and cheap. Sunday was the only day off. Most men worked Monday to Saturday, long hours too, but Sunday was strictly observed. Everywhere was shut apart from the churches. I managed to get into the church choir. I got a halfcrown (2/6d) for the church services each Sunday; 3/6d (18p) for weddings and funerals. I even got time off school for midweek services.

The streets were lit by gaslights and the lamplighter would come around every night and with the aid of a long pole, turn them on, returning the next morning to switch them off. He was a very important man at that time and I remember him cycling up with a ladder on his shoulders to replace any mantles that needed to be changed. He would also clean the glass or repair any broken panes that we kids had damaged during our games. We never did it on purpose though. If we were caught or reported by a neighbour, it would cost my mother a shilling, a lot of money in those days and I would end up with a whack from the old man when he got home. We soon learnt to take care and with the average wage only two pounds per week we could ill afford any unnecessary expenditure. Luxuries were out. Dad made me a bike from old spare parts. It only had a front brake; I had to put my foot on the back tyre to help it stop. I never owned a handkerchief, I had to make do with a bit of Dad's old shirt-tail or a bit of ripped sheet. Holidays were non existent. The best we could expect would be a day out somewhere, to the Botanical Gardens or the Lickey Hills near Bromsgrove. On a rare occasion, or if Dad had got lucky on the horses, we would go on the train to Rhyl or Weston-Super-Mare for the day. Pocket money was out of the question. We would earn money by running errands for the elderly or anyone else willing to spare a copper or two. I used to fetch coal from the coal yard in fourteen and twenty-eight pound sacks. The wheelbarrow I used was heavier than the coal I carried. I would earn a penny a trip and make about 6d to 8d (3p) in a night. I would then go home and give my wages to Mom and she would usually give me a penny back. We all knew our parents found it hard to cope and needed any extra money they could get. The lads in the street would get together and each spend a penny buying a different comic and we would all swop when we had finished until we had read the lot. We did the same with books too. Our parents would never let us take our comics up with us to read in bed and although they never admitted it, as soon as we had gone upstairs, they used to read them themselves. We never threw them away either. When we had finished with them, we took all the books and comics down to the

'Swop Shop' in Ledsam Street, to exchange for some we hadn't yet read. We made sure that we stretched our cash to the limit.

My best mate was Sid. We were always looking for an idea to bring in some extra cash. On one occasion, we got some work at 'Hickmans' down at the fruit and poultry market in St Edwards Street, now the site of the National Indoor Arena. It was a very popular place to shop. We would help tidy up at the end of the day for a few pennies. The boss said we could keep all the old empty, wooden fruit crates. It was all wooden boxes then, no cardboard. We put a rope around them and dragged them home. It took ages. It was nearly two miles. It was worth it in the end. The lot was taken to the back garden where we would take out all the nails and carefully straighten them, then chop up the boxes into sticks to make bundles of firewood. Friday was payday, so on that night we went round the neighbourhood selling them, a halfpenny per bundle and the nails to those who wanted them. It was all coal fires then, so we had a ready market and soon had regular orders for so many bundles each week.

Sometimes we would bring back a big bag of damaged oranges or specked apples. These were very welcome amongst the lads. We never stole anything. We always asked; it was a kind of code of honour; never bite the hand that feeds you. We always got more because of it as well. Three of the lads' Dads worked as stokers or drivers on the trains down the shunting yards. When they were on duty we used to go down with some old sugar or potato sacks and wait at the back of the fence and taunt them as they went by. They would throw lumps of coal at us, over the fence. We would quickly collect them up and put them in our bags and scamper home as soon as they were full.

There was a fruit and vegetable shop on the Ladywood Road and the owner used to have orders from the posh houses in Edgbaston. They would never fetch it themselves; it had to be delivered. That was my job. I was twelve and would do a paper round every morning and evening and then do my deliveries. The goods were loaded into a three wheeled, high-sided basket trolley that I would push or drag to the various houses. Some of the drives were a quarter of a mile long and the houses huge. I got four and six (4/6d), twenty-two and a halfpence in today's money, from the greengrocer, plus a few tips and five shillings (25p) from the paper round. I couldn't take any time off. There was a queue of boys ready to step into my shoes. All together with my firewood and errand money, I contributed about a pound per week into the family coffers.

This made quite a difference to the weekly budget. Mom would usually give me a shilling back. I had plenty of spare time then. We didn't have a television or radio. We had a wind up gramophone and only Dad could touch that.

We moved out of Friston Street in 1933 to a new house at Weoley Castle, to one of the massive inter-war council estates being built at the time. Thousands of houses were being constructed under a government programme in an attempt to relieve the overcrowding of the inner city. We were lucky, Mom and Dad had been trying for years to get a bigger place. The six of us lived in that tiny house but there was no alternative. We were allocated a house in Gregory Avenue. I can remember when we were given the keys to look it over; it had big windows, three bedrooms, a decent sized living room, nice kitchen and the main thing, a bathroom with a flush toilet too - fantastic. A back boiler was provided at the rear of the grate, heated by the fire. There was instant hot water. We couldn't believe such luxury. Mom couldn't take it; she broke down into tears, floods of them, she was that happy. Dad was ecstatic as well. He now had a big garden. We were amongst the first families to move in. The roads weren't even finished; the shops were still under construction. The new bus route finished at the edge of the estate, about one and a half miles away. We were glad to get out of the cramped conditions of Ladywood, but everything had been so convenient and closeby there. Here, we had to make new friends and the new found freedom and space was hard to get used to. Things eventually settled down, shops were built and the regular delivery services of the milkman, baker, coalman and greengrocer followed, all by horse and cart, although companies like the Co-op started using petrol powered vans. It was around this time that milk was first delivered in milk bottles, rather than being ladled out of the urn into one of Mom's jugs. You paid for it as you got it in Ladywood; we got it on tick at Weoley Castle.

I got a job at Wrensons, the grocers, when I left school in 1934. Ten bob (50p) for a sixty hour week. I was lucky; there were three million unemployed. There was no job security, no unions. The boss ruled and could sack you at the drop of a hat, so you didn't complain. You kept your head down and grafted. Promotion was limited and generally via 'the dead man's shoes' rule, but I got lucky and was given a counter job after three months and a halfcrown per week rise. Just as things seemed to be on the up, my elder sisters Laura and Irene died of tuberculosis or TB, as it was known. I think Irene caught it while we were at Friston

Street, but it was probably ignored as most people suffered with coughs and chest colds then. It was considered normal and the real reason only surfaced when we moved to Weoley Castle and then it was too late. It was awful, we were grief stricken. Mom was inconsolable. It finished her, she never got over it and died, heartbroken, a couple of years later. She was only forty-three. It was really hard. We hadn't realised how much Mom did. It was a real struggle, but we got through. We eventually got into a routine, sharing the household chores. Then my call up papers arrived. That was a real blow to Dad and Vera. How would they manage? It happened so quickly. I passed my medical and was enlisted in the army on 15th August 1940. Vera left school shortly after and got a job at Wrensons, in Castle Square, where I used to work, so that helped a bit. I only had a few days leave before I went off and spent most of that at home trying to tie up loose ends. Dad said they would be okay, but I was still worried for them.

CHAPTER TWO

W e reported to Becketts Park, Leeds, a former teachers training centre, but now the Royal Army Medical Corps (RAMC) Depot, to get kitted out. We were also given our army numbers. Mine was 7385197. You never forget it. At the time of the call up we had little choice as to which branch of the Service we would like to join. A lot of men volunteered before they were called up in an attempt to have some choice. We were put in the branch of Service that needed us the most at that particular time. I remember seeing the same faces at Becketts Park as when I went for my medical. Most of that call up went into the Medical Corps (Medics). I would rather have been in something else, but did it matter? The chaps I was with turned out a very dedicated bunch, no cowards there and one must remember, where there is fighting, there are always the Medics. Amongst other things we were told our motto: 'IN ARDUOUS FIDELIS' - 'FAITHFUL IN DIFFICULTIES'. I didn't realise then how hard that motto would be to keep.

The training was intense and we were taught every aspect of army life; strict discipline, marching, army drill, physical training, everything. We were there for eight weeks and slept on the floor, on mattresses filled with straw. The food was good. I was glad to get regular meals. Some of the others were used to better, so it came as a bit of a shock to them. An officer would always come round and try a small portion of the food and each time say the same word, "Delicious". The duty sergeant would shout, "Any complaints" and, remarkably, there never was. After a few days we ate anything and everything put in front of us, none was ever wasted; those finicky eaters soon forgot their likes and dislikes. I found muscles I didn't know I had. We had to wait a week before we had uniforms, there were none available. The country wasn't geared up for war yet. We went on several route marches, fourteen to twenty miles at a time over the hills and valleys of Wharfdale with a full pack. It certainly sorted a few out. We had some amazing blisters wearing army boots for the first time. Roll call was at six in the morning, then one hour of P.T. before breakfast, rain or shine. The rest of the day was spent doing squad drills and lectures. It was all go. We weren't allowed out of the barracks for the first four weeks. Most of the time was spent polishing our equipment, the rest writing home or playing darts and cards. When we did get out, after passing an inspection at the gate (there was a mirror there and we had to make sure we were properly dressed), we couldn't do much, funds were low and we were miles from anywhere. My pay at that time was ten shillings per week (50p), less a shilling (5p) a week barrack damages, in case a window was broken. One of the things I definitely disliked was guard duty, four hours off and two hours on, for forty-eight hours. It was exhausting, standing at a gate between two and four in the early hours, in the dark, in three foot of snow and the freezing cold. My other main dislike, was the gas chamber. We had to run through to see the affect different types of gas had on us. We weren't allowed to use gas masks either. There was mustard gas, phosgene, the lot. It was vile and made us all sick.

We finished basic training. They said that was the worst bit out of the way. We moved out of the barracks and billeted in some empty houses at Headingly. It was a come down from the comfort of the barracks ~ thirty of us to each house! They were cold and miserable, no heating and only one forty-watt bulb in each room. We were allocated our spaces, me in the loft, sleeping on the floor as usual. We washed and shaved in cold water because that was all there was, unless you boiled some. I cut my top lip and got a huge cold sore on it. I couldn't shave properly because of it, so I grew a moustache and have kept it ever since. I had to get permission. The MO (Medical Orderly) gave me a note. You couldn't do what you liked. The army had to approve everything. The local people were very good, they used to leave coal, packets of tea and sugar, milk and loads of cakes and snacks. They gave us a kettle and even an old teapot. We never found out who put it there. It was there in the morning, on the step when we woke up, I'll always remember their kindness. We continued our training in the parks nearby, the locals loved it and had a great laugh at our expense. We had our meals in a derelict school three miles away. Three times a day we marched the six miles there and back for our food. It didn't matter what the food was like, we ate it all. We all had the same too. It didn't matter who you were in the civvy street, the army brought you all down to the same level. At first they passed plates from the head of the table with varying sized portions, but this didn't work, some had too much, others too little. Inevitably fighting broke out and so they changed the system whereby the cooks, distributed the food from a serving hatch. Then, nobody got enough. You know, I don't ever recall having sliced bread in the army, it was always a chunk cut or torn off the loaf. You never let go of it either or else it disappeared. It was the same with all food; despite everybody moaning about it, the moment you looked away, the food disappeared. No-one knew where it went? We also had potatoes with everything, usually boiled or dehydrated; sometimes in their jackets if there wasn't enough soldiers on spud bashing duty, or 'jankers' as we used to call it. You got jankers if you were put on a charge for being late or perhaps improperly dressed. The food was always washed down with plenty of tea and we drank that no matter how it tasted. Sometimes they put sugar in, most times they didn't and the milk was nearly always the evaporated or condensed type. The cooks used a paraffin rag to clean the urn, it was supposed to get rid of the staining, but the after effects used to show up on the top of the tea. I can still remember that smell of paraffin and the rainbow pattern floating on the top. We drank it, moaning like hell, but we had just finished our PT and would have drunk anything.

At night we used to get a tram ride into Leeds. We would have the usual crawl round the pubs and play darts, then to the 'Sally Ann' (Salvation Army) for free beans on toast and a mug of tea. We never had enough money and were always skint and hungry. I even went to church because they offered free tea and sandwiches afterwards; the congregation was about ninety percent servicemen. They didn't pass the plate round, they didn't dare. We had a lot of laughs at that time, with all the chaps settling in, getting to know each other. After we completed our training, we were waiting to be posted, but everything was full of uncertainty owing to the Dunkirk evacuation. We were kitted out to go to Northern Europe somewhere, but that fell through and we were put on permanent standby because of threatened invasion by the Germans.

Then, I was posted to Oxford. I didn't have a diary. In fact, we were told not to keep one in case we got captured. I joined up with the 14th British General Hospital (BGH) there. They were a smashing bunch of lads that had been evacuated from France and were being reformed at Oxford. The local Masonic Hall was used for our billet and the school opposite used as a hospital and training centre. We went to work on the surgical wards and were kept very busy handling the Dunkirk cases. It was a real eye opener; some were in a dreadful state. I worked for Major Moffett, he was a specialist in ear, nose and throat cases and also for Col. Smellie, who in civvy street was the Medical Officer for Birmingham and Chief Medical Consultant at Selly Oak Hospital, Birmingham. I learnt a lot from them and quickly too. Then I had my real surgical training with Col. Kelman, who used to be Chief Surgeon at Selly Oak Hospital. He was excellent, toe nails to amputations, he did the lot. The 14th BGH had been formed in Selly Oak, a territorial unit before the war and consisted mainly of Birmingham lads, but to get the unit up to full strength we drafted in a contingent of Welsh chaps and that worked well. We often played each other up and sometimes had the odd punch up. I really did get a lot of medical training. There were loads of lectures and exams too. It was hard, but I was pleased to hear I had come top, I got ninety three percent in the exam and that meant I was a tradesman Class I. That was pretty good for me and it meant more pay as well, not a lot, but it was a start.

I had my first leave in January 1941, only five days, but Dad and Vera were pleased to see me. We had a lot to talk about as it was five months since I had joined up and I had been worried about how they were managing. Dad tried to reassure me they were all right, but I was still concerned. I couldn't do much about it, I had to go back to my unit the following Sunday. During the next few months I did a lot of training inside and out of the Unit, mainly down south. I went to various Casualty Clearing Stations, Field-posts, Mobile Operating Theatres, MI rooms, everything to do with the casualties of war in the field, including preparing and issuing necessary paperwork to accompany them, so that their unit and more importantly, their next of kin knew what was going on. I also went to Dalkeith in Scotland for two weeks, attached to a Highland Brigade, teaching some of their own men how to set up and run a field post. Eventually, I went back to Oxford and did night duty for a time, one month on and one month off. I was put in charge of a thirty-bed ward, full of post tonsil operations. That certainly kept me busy. During any time off, I would go with my mates boating on the local River Isis, or to the local pubs and dances, even tours around the colleges. We used to do firewatching on the roofs of the colleges at night and I actually got to know my way around by the roofs of various college blocks. Things remained the same for a while, but there were always constant rumours about where we were going. Being a field hospital we knew we would be on the move as soon as possible, but to where? Twice we were kitted out for overseas, only to have to hand it all back. Everything seemed uncertain, then all of a sudden we were finally told that we were to be on the move. I managed to get a forty eight hour leave pass and rushed to get home by Saturday lunch time, but had to be back by 23.59 hours on Sunday night, so there was no time to waste.

It was 4th December, 1941 when the Colonel addressed the Parade and told us we were to go overseas. It was definite this time. We were examined by the MO for overseas service and given lots of inoculations for the various tropical diseases we might encounter. Then, we were moved out of our billets to Cowley, just outside Oxford, but the only accommodation available to us was in a dance hall that had been taken over by the Army. We slept on the floor, but it was a sprung floor and every time someone walked by, you would bounce up and down. We were sworn to secrecy as to where we might be going. None of us knew anyway. Another unit had taken over from us at the hospital and we were

With Vera during my first leave

put on standby to move at an hour's notice. It was quite tense. Then it all went quiet again, the urgency was no longer there and we thought it was another false alarm. In the meantime, I went to various ordnance depots checking equipment which would be assembled and sent with us when, or if, we were sent abroad. Then, we were granted seven days leave. I went home. I had no time to tell Dad or Vera, but they were obviously pleased to see me. I did explain it was probably embarkation leave and I would soon be on my way, so we made the best of it. I had only spent four days at home when a telegram arrived telling me to report back to Oxford immediately. I said my goodbyes and returned on 30th December 1941. There was no New Year's Eve celebration with the family. We were confined to the barracks from then on until early on Sunday 4th January 1942 when we boarded the train at Oxford. The Brummies amongst us couldn't believe it when the train arrived at Snow

Hill Station, Birmingham. We couldn't go anywhere though, the station was sealed off and the phones cut too. The main reason was that the unit was mainly made up of local lads and the authorities thought they may let their families know they were on the move. Then we found out the reason for our stop, the army catering corps had set up a meal on the station platform. We quickly ate that and then got back onto the train. It was then non-stop until we reached the Liverpool Docks, then straight off the train onto our troopship, the M.V. Britannic. The Britannic was a huge liner, still in civvy order, just as it was for the luxury cruises it used to take before the war. It wasn't that old really. It had been launched in 1929 and was the last of the White Star Line, used on the Liverpool to New York cruise run. It was used as a troopship from 1939 to 1947 before reverting back to civvy use. There were some basic improvements made to the Britannic to facilitate its wartime operation and some of these included six inch guns, erected fore and aft, plus other weapons. We were not to be treated to too much luxury. It was six men to a cabin meant for two, with only two beds. We worked it out though; two men in the separate beds, the rest on the floor, but agreed to change about each week, so everybody had a bed at one time or another. More troops came on board next day. It was packed. There were now about three thousand men on the ship and it was queues for everything, the toilets being the worst. Meals were in relays. I don't know how the cooks managed, but the food was good.

No one knew where we were going. We had all been issued with Arctic gear and assumed we were going to Northern Europe. We weren't allowed to post any mail, although we could write and put it in the ship's post box, but this wouldn't be sent anywhere until we had got to where we were going. We moved out of Liverpool on 6th January and went to the Clyde area of Scotland, where more of the convoy was starting to assemble. No ship travelled alone because of U-boat attacks. We had lost a lot of ships and men through them. We were to be part of a convoy of twenty four ships sailing through the Atlantic at a critical time of the war, knowing German 'U' boats were out in packs and very active. It was not a pleasant thought. We were in the Clyde for four days when late on the Sunday evening, we felt the boat start moving. We were off. We didn't know what was happening or where we were going.

When we boarded the ship at Liverpool, all the troops were issued with hammocks and those that were not in cabins were told to sleep in them. Ropes were hung from the roof of the hold and you were supposed to tie one end to one rope and the other end to another rope a short distance away, climb up the rope and get into your hammock. You now were about fifteen feet above the deck or floor and of course no-one had a clue what they were doing, let alone had any experience of trying to sleep in a hammock. The navy ones are just about long enough to get in to and lie straight out, flat on your back. You couldn't move without fear of falling out and it was impossible to turn over; you were far too scared to go to sleep. In the night, bodies would be heard hurtling down onto the deck with a hell of a smack, or on top of the troops who were lying on the floor underneath because they were too scared to use the hammocks. A body falling some fifteen feet on to them caused quite a bit of aggro. In the end it had to be abandoned, the movement of the ship, especially in the North Atlantic. The hammocks were moving about like giant pendulums and nearly everybody was seasick, so the last place to be sleeping was underneath a hammock.

Moving about on the ship was really difficult in the bad weather. You would try to open a door and it didn't budge, so you put your shoulder against it and again nothing happened. Suddenly, it would open with a hell of a rush and you find yourself hanging on to the ship's rails looking down at the ocean below. It's a wonder I never went over the side. It was the same trying to get downstairs. You would force one foot in front of the other, then suddenly, you would be lying in a heap at the bottom as the ship moved from beneath you. You could never walk in a straight line. Even drinking a mug of tea was a problem at first. You would get it as far as your lips and find it slopping over the other side of the mug or over you. We eventually found our sea legs in the end, by which time we were near Iceland in the North Atlantic Ocean, on the way to Canada. The weather was diabolical, it was so cold and windy, really bleak. The huge mountainous waves made the ship go up and down like a cork, making the boat do everything except turn over and I couldn't think why it didn't. On top of that, we had really fatty bacon for breakfast and belly of pork at mid-day. Oh boy, that certainly turned the seasickness on. Everybody seemed to be affected. They were sick all over the place. I was all right at first, then some idiot was sick all over my plate, just as I sat down to eat. That was it; that started me off, it was terrible. I joined the rest of the bodies lying about the place. We didn't want to move, just curl up and die. I was still ill the next day, but was called up to the operating theatre to assist with an emergency appendix operation. I did the best I could, but we all felt awful, even the surgeon was sick. We all had a cup of Bovril after we had finished, but I hadn't eaten for two days, so as soon as I drank it, I immediately fetched it back up. It was hopeless, you couldn't keep anything down. I had no food for nearly five days, but afterwards, when I felt a little better, I couldn't get enough, I was ravenous.

Now, there were about forty ships in the convoy, including two battleships, the Ramilles and the Revenge, destroyers and corvettes, escorting the other troopships and us to wherever we were going. We still didn't know. Many of the troopships at that time were converted famous passenger liners of the day and there were several in the convoy, such as the Stirling Castle, the Windsor Castle, Le Pasteur and the Britannic, which we were on. It was a very impressive sight and a target for U-boats. I think we were about five hundred miles out from the UK when a Focke-Wülf German long-range aircraft spotted us. The convoy fired everything at it, but it kept out of range and went away, to report our position. We then expected to be attacked by U-boats, German submarines. They hunted in packs. So, the whole convoy altered course and went full speed towards Canada and out of range of any possible air or U-boat attack. Whilst in the danger areas, all the ships travelled in a zig-zag fashion, going nine minutes one way and nine minutes the other way. The reason, we were told, was that it takes a U-boat ten minutes to line up and fire a torpedo, so we should be all right. All the ships travelled with no lights. We had to take turns on lookout duty, two of us at a time, on different parts of the ship. Me and this other chap had to do our watch at the stern of the boat, from 2.00 am to 4.00 am. It was a real cold and misty night. You couldn't see much at all and it was so cold you could hardly move. Suddenly, out of the mist, loomed the huge bow of the Stirling Castle, only a few yards away. It was about to hit us. We immediately sounded the alarm and the crew sped into action flashing lights and giving signals to alert the other ship. There wasn't any panic, they were well-drilled professionals, but everyone gave a sigh of relief when it eventually moved slowly away. It would have been very serious had there been a crash, especially in those weather conditions; no-one would have had a chance if they went in the water. Life on board was getting tedious. We were confined below decks because of the atrocious weather. The waves were coming over the decks of the ship and it was freezing cold. We still had the usual lifeboat drill. They were very strict, there was no nonsense. We were allocated sections of the deck which we had to go to when the alarm was sounded and no-one was allowed to get into the life boats until told to do so. Machine guns were positioned round the rails, and we were told anyone moving out of line or causing panic would be shot. They actually meant it. When you think about it, you need discipline to try and get thousands of men off a sinking ship. Any panic would cause a catastrophe.

We had been to Iceland and Canada, refuelled and still we kept going, yet we had no idea where we were. We noticed it was starting to get warmer and by the 21st January it was getting hot. The area must have been safe because the order went out for us to start washing our clothes - socks and things. There were bits of string and rope everywhere with washing hanging out to dry all over the place. We could spend more time on deck. Conditions were starting to get a little more pleasant at last. On 25th January, a shout went up, "Land ahoy". Everybody rushed on deck. In the distance, just above the horizon, we could see the tops of trees and gradually, land came into sight. A few of the lads took some wild guesses about were we where, mostly wrong of course. It turned out to be Freetown, Sierra Leonne, on the coast of West Africa. It was a tremendous sight seeing the ships scattered about the bay. We were told three ships had been lost on the way over; two ammunition boats and a store ship. From the Britannic, we saw the ammo boat go up one night. It was blown to bits. There was not a chance of any survivors. In fact, we were told a convoy never stopped to pick anyone up, whether the enemy hit them or someone fell overboard. The risk would be too great for the rest on board. One or two chaps on our ship went overboard, but there was no rescue attempt. The destroyers had a quick look. It must have been awful for the poor men in the water, left to drown and with the knowledge that no-one would come back for them.

Only a few of us were allowed ashore at Freetown. It couldn't absorb all the troops, but it wasn't the cleanest place either and there was a lot of tropical disease there at that time. The last thing the authorities wanted was it to infect the men. I was one of the 'lucky ones' chosen. In fact, I went two days running, helping to get medical supplies. I also visited the local hospital. It was very primitive by our standards, but it was all they had, so they made do as best they could. The whole area of Freetown was very backward. It was not a nice place at all; very hot, humid, swampy; typically tropical. They called it the white man's grave and it wasn't difficult to see why. On board ship it was scorching hot, there was no air movement at all and millions of flies descended on us. We couldn't keep them away. They got everywhere. The locals came out in small boats, or

Bum-boats as they were called, laden with fresh fruit and nuts. They would send a basket up on a rope for you to put your money in, you would then lower it down and tell them what you wanted and then pull it back up. They were very honest about it and the fruit made a refreshing change. We were issued with tropical kit. It was in the hold of the ship. We'd had no idea it was there. We thought we were going north. We all looked a right bunch of comics in our long shorts and Royal Marine type hats and although we had a good laugh at first, we soon got used to our new attire. It was much more practical.

We left Freetown after four days. The Royal Marines played the convoy out from the deck of one of the warships there. We weren't sorry to go. It had been so hot, day and night, in that still air and we got little sleep. We would be much better off on the move. We had the sea breeze. Now the weather was warmer, we were allowed to sleep on deck. It was a lot more comfortable. We saw shoals of fish, porpoises and a lot of sharks. The sharks used to follow the ship waiting for the waste food and scraps to be thrown overboard. This was done at dusk in case enemy ships saw the debris on the water, but I didn't think that was necessary, as the sharks soon made short work of it. It was fascinating to watch them. They left nothing, not a thing. We also saw schools of flying fish and couldn't believe that they really did fly; they used their fins like wings. It was such a fantastic sight.

It was Saturday 31st January when we crossed the Equator and the crew made quite a ceremony of it. King Neptune, one of the senior crew members, held court and I was one of the victims. His helpers lathered me up with an outsize shaving brush and then shaved me with a huge wooden razor and then threw me over the side of the ship. I was fished out and received a signed Certificate off King Neptune to say I was a member of his Court and would not be molested if ever I crossed the Equator again.

The next few days were very hot and sticky, everybody slept on deck with just the sea to look at. On the sixth day it got a little cooler and the sea started getting rough. We soon found out why, we were about to go around the Cape of Good Hope at the bottom tip of Africa. It was the early part of February when we rounded the Cape and the convoy started to split up, some to Durban, some to Cape Town. We went to Cape Town, but only stayed a short time, just enough for a quick sight-see, from the boat of course. We didn't go ashore. Then we continued to Durban. It was Friday 13th February, a journey of some fifteen days from Freetown, the last time my feet touched dry land. For others it must have been worse. We seemed to have been on board ship forever. We were given shore leave at Durban, but had to be back on board ship no later than 23.59 hours, with no exceptions and that included officers. You could face a court martial if you weren't back. It was wonderful to put your feet on firm ground, but it did take a while to get used to it. We wobbled all over the place at first. The white South Africans were really pleased to see us. They came to the dock area in their cars every morning and took us sightseeing and even into their homes for meals. They couldn't do enough for us. The Town Hall was filled with food and fruit and other refreshments. It was all free as well, all day long. We couldn't believe it. One day, me and a few of the lads had been invited to see the shark fishing, so we took a steam train to a place called Amanzimtoti on the coast and went out on a lovely yacht. We were there all day and at night we were treated to a slap up meal and dance. We didn't pay for a thing, our hosts saw to that. I'll never forget how kind and considerate they were. The rest of the time we took it easy and would just sight-see around the local area, perhaps going to a fruit orchard to see pineapples, oranges and grapes being grown. We weren't used to this. We had only ever seen them at the market or in the shops. I would like to go back there someday. Of course, they had apartheid there. We weren't used to that either; a different section of a place for blacks and a different section for whites. A bus or tram had separate entries, separate seats and that's how it was, right through the entire system; even in parks, seats for whites and seats for blacks. The whites did not mix with blacks and vice-versa.

On our last day in Durban we changed ships and transferred to the Strathnaver, a large, three funnelled, former P&O liner, built for the London to Sydney run and specially adapted for the tropical seas. Although it was larger than the Britannic, the conditions were not as good. We had four thousand men on board and toilets for only three hundred, most of which had tummy upsets through eating too much fruit and foreign food. There was mess everywhere, no time to queue. It was disgusting. They had to hose the decks down every hour, it was that bad. On the last day in Durban we had all got back to the ship, and had just finished roll call at midnight when we felt the boat start moving. We were off. We assumed we were going to Singapore, but what we didn't know was that Singapore had been overrun by the Japs and we were on our way there, in a last ditch attempt at a rescue operation. A change of mind must have taken place because after two days out from Durban, a destroyer approached the convoy and messages were passed to and fro, and there was a lot of flag waving (because of the radio blackout) as the messages were passed around the convoy. The order was given for the whole convoy to turn round. Singapore had collapsed on 15th February 1942. Obviously a rescue attempt would be of no use.

I lost count of how many days we had spent on the water. There was no land in sight, it was just very hot and sticky all the time. We lay on deck all day, drinking tea at two pence (2d) a pint. We were all sunburnt and very bored. We had read all the books we had and told all the jokes we knew. We would have loved a lovely pint of beer, ice cold, that would have just done the trick, but all troopships were dry, which meant no alcohol. So we just had to accept it and wait. Land was sighted, but where were we? It turned out to be Ceylon. We all thought great, this will do us until the end of the war, but no such luck, we only spent two days there. It was a smashing place, but it appeared they didn't want us. There wasn't enough room. It was already overcrowded with other troops, so away we went. Things started to get rough on the ship, the heat was beginning to get very oppressive, the food seemed to be getting worse and the water was restricted to drinking only. We had to wash with sea water. It was hopeless, even with the special salt-water soap. Then, the Medical Officer condemned all the flour on board. Apparently it was full of cockroaches, so it was all thrown over the side. It was then down to bully beef and biscuits, the latter being as tough as concrete. You couldn't bite them. They had to be nibbled. They wouldn't even soften in tea. We were given less water and started to get anxious. It appeared that Ceylon could not supply us with food or water. They had none to spare. We all wondered where we would land up and more importantly, when? We seemed to have spent a long time at sea but had no destination. The ship thumped its way on and then on 9th March, land was once again sighted. It turned out to be Bombay, India. We anchored in the harbour and wondered whether this was the end of our journey. The next day we pulled into the landing stage. We were pleased to reach land. We had started our journey from the England on 4th January and finished at Bombay on 11th March 1942, a total of sixty-seven days or just over nine weeks. We were given two days shore leave and we all had a good look round. When you have been on a ship for such a long time, it really does take a couple of days to get used to walking again on land, you sway all over the place. Bombay was a real shock, a huge contrast to England. We had never seen anything like it before. Typically, we all went round the places we were told not to visit and had a great laugh. Crowds of Indians followed us everywhere, begging, "Buckshees Sahib", but we hadn't got any money ourselves. We eventually went back to the ship. At that time we did not know what was happening. We had no idea what was taking place in Europe, Asia or anywhere. It was just as well. What we did find out when we finally reached India, was that the convoy had been re-routed from Singapore to Java, but because the Japs were advancing so fast, the convoy was again re-routed to India. There was so much chaos; they didn't know what to do with us.

CHAPTER THREE

I t was the evening of the 14th March 1942 when we left the ship and boarded the train to Lucknow. We travelled on that train for two days and arrived at Lucknow on the afternoon of the 16th March. It was so hot, especially on the train and the scenery wasn't much to look at either, flat and barren. We weren't impressed with India. At that time, we were all on emergency rations and we had to wait for the train to stop before we could make a brew of tea. Then, one of us would rush up to the engine and the driver would fill our urns with boiling water. There was no fresh milk, just tinned, evaporated or condensed. The tea tasted horrible, but at least it was at least a drink and free from germs. At Lucknow we were allotted some old British pre war barracks. We could hire bearers for eight annas per week (about 4p). They cleaned our boots, made the beds, attended to our washing, in fact, anything we wanted them to do. We thought we had hit the jackpot and made the best of it while we could, we knew it wouldn't last. The food was good. We had our own cooks. We were all pleased about that. We had been served some right rubbish since we left Durban. The weather was very hot during the day and only slightly cooler at night and although uncomfortable, this spell in Lucknow gave us a chance to acclimatise and adjust our bodies to the different way of life.

The Colonel in charge put us all on parade and said we shouldn't be there at all. We were supposed to have gone to Singapore. They didn't expect us and no-one seemed to know what to do with, so we sat back and enjoyed the good life and went sightseeing. Lucknow was a large town and there was plenty to see. I went to where Clive of India fought the rebels when the siege of Lucknow took place. The bazaars were the places to be. You could put your feet on a piece of leather and a fellow would draw round it and measure your foot with a piece of string. Two hours later, you could get a pair of shoes, all leather and really cheap too. It was the same with clothing, measured in the morning and collected at four in the afternoon, all for just a few rupees.

It seemed to get hotter daily. It was over one hundred degrees in the shade. We were issued with mosquito nets, but the flies had long teeth and spiked boots. If you didn't pull the nets down at night for protection, you didn't sleep and you got covered in lumps, minus a pint of blood. You soon got into the habit of using the net after that. A lot of lads were going down with dysentery because they did not take enough precautions with the water and ate the food in the local cafes. We were all warned, but some men didn't seem to bother.

I spent two weeks in Lucknow. At the end of March I went with an advance party to a place called Bareilly in the United Provinces, based at another peacetime barracks. We were told it was a punishment centre for British troops that had misbehaved. It was situated on the plains of India, very hot, just like a desert, with flat barren land for miles around. There was only a small regimental canteen, a small church and a tin hut for a cinema for when they got a film and that was on very rare occasions. That was it; the local village was just one street and all the British troops were confined to a containment area. The main town of Bareilly was out of bounds because it was the headquarters for the Indian Congress Party and supported the Gandhi riots and resistance that was rife in India at that time. The British Army didn't want to get involved in any trouble and so kept the troops away. I did manage to visit it. Four of us dressed up in dhotis, with two Anglo-Indians to do all the talking. We had a good look round, just for the hell of it. It was silly because if the locals found out, we would have been stabbed to death, but I'm glad I went.

Things were not good in Burma at that time, the British had retreated and there were a lot of casualties, but very little in the way of medical care. No-one has been prepared for it. The Japanese attacked with such speed and surprise. The British Army fought a rear guard action but was completely surprised. After the invasion more British and Indian troops were rushed into Burma to help but time and distance were against them and so were the thick jungle conditions. Soon Rangoon fell and all supplies had to come overland from India. The Japs pushed our troops back to the Indo-Burma border and there was chaos as soldiers and civilians tried to escape. They didn't take prisoners. Any British or Indian troops were shot. So were the civilians who were not fit enough or refused to work for them. Anything of value was taken, including livestock and food, to feed the Japanese troops. This was the reason they advanced so quickly, they didn't need to wait for supplies. British troops were singled out for special atrocious treatment and it became impossible to leave any wounded behind. The Japs would cut their throats, or torture and bayonet them. Those wounded that couldn't be moved were better off being shot by our own troops. That happened too. Pals couldn't bear to see their friends suffer, so they shot them. The retreating troops reached Imphal in May 1942.

At that time our unit had taken over the small British Military Hospital which was in Bareilly. It had been there in the peacetime years. There were only thirty beds, but it was run really well. Bearers did all the manual work. I was sent to help out there but only to supervise. That suited me. The rest of the unit was turning any available barracks into wards to make it into a twelve hundred-bed hospital. They also took over the little military hospital where I was working and turned it into an 'officers only' ward. The hospital was ready for operation by May 12th. The theatre was brick built and very well equipped. The wards were up to date. We received two hundred patients the first day it opened, more the next day and so it continued. The hospital was working at full capacity in next to no time. Most of the patients were in a bad way. They had not received proper attention on the way to us and it was a hell of a journey from Burma. The 14th British General Hospital was the most up to date in India with top rate surgeons and medical officers. We had good, British sisters who really knew their job and a very high percentage of the other ranks were top quality in their different fields. They needed to be. Most of the staff did a twelve-hour shift, day or night; every day. There was no let up. I worked in the operating theatre mainly, but I did surgical dressings on the wards when time permitted. I liked the surgical work best. You could see the results of your endeavours.

We couldn't believe it would get any hotter, but it did. It was now over one hundred and ten degrees in the shade. A lot of our chaps were going down with heat exhaustion and dysentery. The bad news was that we were told it would get a lot worse; May, June and July were the hottest months. The heat was the main topic of conversation. As it got worse there seemed no difference between day and night. The heat was unbearable. I put a thermometer outside and it registered over one hundred and twenty degrees. We all suffered from prickly heat and that made it hard to lie down. The sweat just poured out of you continuously. The

Len 3rd from left, 2nd row from back, with the other British lads that ran the IGH

army tried to relieve the situation and all the wards and barracks were fitted with punkas. These were queer contraptions, similar to carpets fitted sideways, on a frame suspended from the ceiling. They went backwards and forwards, driven by an electric motor to attempt to fan the areas below. There would be as many as twenty of these in one ward or barrack room and the noise was awful, as they squeaked and groaned non stop, but all they really did was push the hot air about, so it was still as bad. The ground was rock hard and there wasn't a blade of grass in sight. It was so hot, you could hardly focus your eyes. Everything shimmered and looked hazy. We didn't see a cloud for weeks and it felt as if something was draining all the strength from your body. Then, to make conditions worse, there was a very strong wind called the 'Loo'. This preceded the monsoon and combined with the heat, made you feel as though you were being sandblasted; face, arms, legs, anything exposed, all got very sore. No one was allowed out without wearing a hat, in fact, the CO (Commanding Officer) said unless it was essential, no-one was to go out at all between 10.30am and 4.00pm. We exchanged our huge hats for much lighter ones and our long shorts for a shorter pair. It wasn't much, but we felt and looked a lot better for it. When we took our boots off at night, they would be curled up the next morning because all the moisture had dried out of them. We had a hell of a job getting them on again, so we used to put the leg of the bed into the boots and a large stone on the toe caps, it was the only way to keep them straight. Sometimes we could get a rock cake from the cookhouse, but if you forgot to eat it and left it beside the bed while you went to sleep, ants would appear from nowhere and set about it. When you touched the cake the next morning, it would disappear into a cloud of dust; the ants had sucked every scrap of moisture out of it.

On one occasion I woke up in the night and found a scorpion on my right forearm. Before I had time to do anything it stung me. The pain was excruciating and my arm swelled up almost immediately. My mates rushed me to the M.I. room and I was given a shot of morphine to ease the pain. My arm was put in a sling and I was excused duties for twelve days, it took that long to get better. I thought I could do nothing and was looking forward to the rest, but no such luck. Some twit let on that I was left handed, so I had to do some light work in the company office.

Six of us were posted to Allahabad. The Americans were building a huge air base there and scores of them were going down with heat stroke and heat exhaustion. They told us they were dying at the rate of twelve a week and the local hospital couldn't cope. Our CO sent us to help out and told us to do something about it; uphold the name of the 14th BGH. So, we set up a heat stroke and heat exhaustion unit, plus a dysentery unit and we made a very good job of it too. The Yanks were well pleased and the colonel in charge came and thanked us personally and invited us into the officers' mess for a meal. We were chuffed to death and gratefully accepted. It was great - a huge steak and all the trimmings. We hadn't had a meal like that for some time. We should have stayed there for four weeks and would have done so with pleasure, but our CO cancelled it. Apparently, ninety of our own unit was on the sick list and we had to return to Bareilly to fill in. It appeared that our lads had a spate of heat exhaustion, dysentery, septic prickly heat, boils and other ailments that were rife in those climatic conditions. We had only stayed in Allahabad for eight days and the temperature was one hundred and twenty degrees plus. Imagine working outside on an airfield in that heat. No wonder so many fell ill. The first thing we had to do on our return was to set up another heat and exhaustion centre.

It was almost the end of June before the rains came. When the monsoon broke everybody rushed outside naked, dancing. The cooling effect was utter relief. We saw some terrific thunderstorms. They lasted for three days and nights, non-stop; it was like a firework display; we had never seen rain like it. The ground however, was so hard it couldn't absorb the water and there were floods everywhere. Even the snakes were coming out of their holes to try to get to drier places. We were told to be very careful and check our boots before putting them on just in case. One morning I actually killed a two-foot Cobra that tried to find refuge in the barracks. I used my kukri and chopped its head right off. It was all I had at the time. One of the Indians said it was only a baby one, but I can tell you, it was big enough for me. The rains continued for some time and although it was slightly cooler, the atmosphere was very humid and this made you sweat even more, aggravating the prickly heat. The constant itching sent you crazy. It was like a form of torture. In the end, I reported sick. I had several patches of infected prickly heat, plus a couple of boils on my back and was suffering from exhaustion. It was not surprising considering the heat and the hours I had put in. They recommended me for a spell in the hills, at Raniket. It was cooler there. Practically all the unit had been there by now, there were only six of us that hadn't. Now it was my turn for a bit of a rest.

It was the first week of August when I left for Raniket, a mountain village some seven thousand feet above sea level on the lower slopes of the Himalayas. The scenery was fantastic. You could see most of the Himalayan range. The view was breathtaking. I had never seen anything like it. The climate there was completely different. It was a lot cooler, just like Spring in England. We could feel it as soon as we left the plains and started going up into the hills. The prickly heat and other sores soon started to vanish as our bodies began to cool down. The relief was tremendous. I hadn't felt this cool since we were on the ship coming out. It was a wonderful to feel normal again and not suffer the constant itching and irritation that the hot, sticky climate brought. It was quite incredible the change in such a short time and not only the heat either. When we left the plains to go up into the mountains, the scenery was not so barren and gave way to pine trees and forest. There was also a great difference in the animals. On the plains they were very thin with mangy fur, but in the mountains, they were beautiful, their fur in lovely condition and they were well fed too. Not only that, there was more variety, such as wolves, snow leopards, tigers, bears and monkeys. We didn't see that many, but you could hear them, especially at night.

To get to Raniket, we went by train to the railhead at Kathgodam, then by bus along very narrow, treacherous roads, for about seventy miles, climbing all the time. The bus driver carefully negotiated the dangerous curves and steep gradients as we went. This was India and the road only went so far, then became a track and the bus couldn't go any further. So, it was by truck, horse or mule for the rest of the way. Raniket itself was perched on the side of a mountain, a trading centre on the borders of Tibet, dealing mainly in furs. It was quite a primitive place, but there were a lot of bazaar type stalls there and considering it was miles from anywhere there was a good assortment of goods. We stayed there for three weeks. It was the first decent leave I had and so I made the most of it. I went everywhere, to Amritsar, site of the Sikh Holy Temple to Peshawar, the Kyber Pass; I even climbed a mountain. They said it was eleven thousand feet high. I think the most exciting time was had when I went on a pony trek into Tibet. It was vast. I had seen nothing like it anywhere. I know that travelling abroad is more popular nowadays, but then it was restricted to a very privileged few and was virtually unheard of for the people I knew and I think even today, places like Tibet are not regular tourist spots for your average holidaymaker. So, you can imagine how we felt being in places that we hadn't even seen in books. The area around where we stayed was used by the Colonials to send their families during the hot season on the plains during peacetime. We used to get invited to Naini-Tal by the local residents, to the beautiful bungalows on the shore of a lake high up in the mountains. It was very nice, although a bit snobbish for us, having tea and biscuits with the Memsahibs, but they felt they were doing their bit for the war effort and they did treat us very well.

Camel Train through the Kyber Pass

Pony Trekking at Raniket

Another Brummie in Burma

Local Village Scene

Fur Trading Centre at Raniket

Naini Tal

Naini Tal

Horse Riding in Naini Tal 1942

We were feeling much more refreshed after our break and it was a sad feeling when the orders came to return to Bareilly towards the end of August. I reluctantly returned to my unit and back to the uncomfortable hot sticky conditions which were to last until the end of October. Life was varied at that time, I went on survival training and also did a lot of work in the operating theatre. I went on several journeys to other places in India, by air, train and road, taking or fetching equipment and supplies, or setting up heat exhaustion units to deal with the newly arrived troops that were affected. It was most satisfying; I really enjoyed it and also saw a lot more of India. Then on the 30th October I was sent back up into the hills to Naini-Tal. I had to help out at a small British civilian hospital because of staff sickness and also, to help close down the leave centre as it was coming to the end of the season and it was now slightly cooler on the plains. I had a wonderful ten days there and a fair amount of free time. I managed to get on another trek into Tibet again. It was very wild and desolate, nature in the raw, not a sign of civilisation anywhere and fantastic views. I could see the whole of the Himalayan range this time, including Mount Nanda Devi, one of the highest mountains in the world and took some lovely photographs. I would have taken a lot more, but we only had one film. You couldn't get them then. Cameras were easy to get hold of , but films were in very short supply and didn't keep long in that type of climate.

Things were eerie in the hills at night. The jungle seemed to come to life and you would hear all sorts of noises. There were always lots of wolves about. They were a nuisance, scavenging round the bins for scraps of food. They were quite frightening especially if you came face to face with one. The monkeys were pests as well. We couldn't believe it at first. A whole group of them would converge on us as we left the cookhouse to walk to the canteen tent to eat and they would try to steal the food right off our plates. Unfortunately, while we were watching out for them, the kitehawks would fly down and snatch the food with their talons. It became a battle of wits in the end, but we had some great laughs as we watched the new intake of troops suffer as we did. Of course, we all learnt how to deal with it the hard way and must have looked hilarious as we trooped out of the cookhouse with our hats over our food, kicking out at the monkeys. The kitehawks were large birds with about a five foot wing span, capable of picking up a small animal, so the pastime with some of the chaps was to tie a stone on a piece of string with a piece of meat on the other end. The hawks would zoom down, pick up the meat with the stone attached and fly off to a fair height to eat. Of course when they had done so they would drop the remains and down would come the stone. The CO put a stop to it in the end after one had hit him.

I returned to Bareilly on 9th November, to be greeted with rumours that the hospital was moving. New and different medics started to move in and also an American unit came to us for further training. They were a great bunch of chaps, we really got on well with them. The Rajputtan Regiment training centre was also nearby and we used to play them at football and cricket. They invited us to their mess for a real Indian meal; that made a nice change from the regular army food. Our unit had a very good cricket team and we played against other Regiments. We won the Regimental Cup and I was in the team; I'm proud of that. It was quite a perk really because we travelled to places that we would not normally see. Incidentally, all sports played in the hot season took place early in the morning or late in the evening. There were no floodlights then, so the game had to be completed before it got dark.

Christmas 1942 was spent in Bareilly. There were no parties or celebrations as such, no booze, nothing, it was just a normal day for us. We were waiting for General Headquarters (GHQ) to make up their mind and let us know where and when we were going. I had been lucky. I had been out and about quite a lot, but some of the chaps hadn't even been out of the camp area. They were fed up. Some would dress up at night in their best uniform, walk up and down the village street, but there was nothing there, so they ended up shouting abuse at each other. That was their night out. My pay at that time was only one pound nine shillings and sixpence (£1.47) per week, paid in Rupees, so I couldn't afford to go out every night. Our money went further over there, so it wasn't that bad, but we were still skint most of the time. One of the other biggest moans was the mail, or rather the lack of it. It came once a month at best. In my own case, I had only received three letters in twelve months. I know they were being sent but they just didn't arrive. There was no airmail then. It all came by sea and we assumed it must be getting sunk. It appears that the U-boat activity in the Atlantic, plus Gandhi and his civil disobedience, together with the Japs, put mail at the bottom of the list. At home, Dad and Vera got their first letter from me in the second week of May. It must have been awful for them as I had left on 4th January and they had no idea where I was. They then knew I was with the South East Asia Command, but didn't know the actual place. Dad thought I was in North Africa somewhere.

We started getting a lot of terrible thunderstorms. They lasted for days and there were floods everywhere. It was all part of the monsoon of course, so we weren't too bothered. Despite the conditions, there were some advantages with the monsoon. The weather was cooler and that made life more tolerable. You still had to get on with the job in hand, whatever the weather. There was a war on. Three of us did a course in blood transfusion techniques and set up a mobile unit to serve the area. It was very interesting and much needed, but our mates called us the 'Vampire Squad'. We didn't mind though, it was all in good fun. There were down times too. One of our lads, Private Duffy had died from Weil's disease. Apparently, he caught it from being in contact with in-fected rat urine. He was older than us, in fact quite a bit older, forty-two. He was buried with full military honours at the small British cemetery in Bareilly. I was one of the bearers there.

When the opportunity arose, I would travel about, anything to escape the monotony of camp life. I went to the Jumna River, a branch of the Ganges. It was an interesting spot, quite scenic, a lot of rice grew there. I could see the funeral pyres on the banks of the river. It was really strange, the old people lived in a tent, next to this heap of wood, on which they would be eventually burned after they had died and their

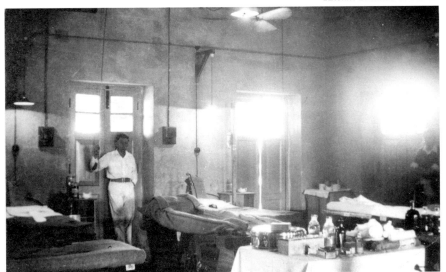

Blood Tranfusion (Vampire) Unit

ashes thrown into the river. This seemed incredible to me, but I was told that it was all part of their religion. I also visited a nomad village nearby. It was very primitive and they brought out their idol for us to see. We even watched a crocodile being caught, a very large specimen indeed. It was getting old and had been causing a lot of trouble attacking the villagers so they had to get rid of it.

A trip to the Juama River

Local Indians with their Idol

Crocodile caught in the Jumna River

Another stroke of luck came my way, I had been chosen to go on an organised trip to visit Agra and see the Taj Mahal. They got the money out of an educational fund, but we didn't care, we took anything that came along. Fifteen of us set out from Bareilly at 8.30 am on the Wednesday and arrived at nine thirty the next morning, sleeping on the train. After we had arrived, we went to special leave barracks for a wash and meal, then to visit the Fort at Agra. It was a fantastic place with three palaces, one of which was completely made of marble. It was real eerie underground. There was a system of dungeons, torture chambers and other such places. I thought that they must have been a wicked lot in the past, no nonsense then, just the chop and straight into the river which ran under the fort. We travelled on to see the Taj Mahal, a short distance from the fort. It was marvellous, past description. I remember thinking I would like all my family to see this. On the Friday we went to the deserted city of Fatehpur Sikri. They told us it was once the capital of India and Akbar the Great used to reside there. It was a long way from anywhere and very hot and barren, over one hundred degrees in the shade, but the reason it was empty was that all the water had suddenly dried up. A huge lake had vanished, caused by an earthquake. No one lived there although there were a lot of visitors, but they had to take their own water. We also went to Sikandra where Akbar the Great was buried in a mausoleum and that was another wonderful sight. A lot of the chaps used to spend any free time they had 'on the town', drinking and chasing what women were about. Although I did my fair share, we couldn't do that where we were. These were sacred places. There were Redcaps everywhere. I liked to see the country, take in the sights and culture. I had spent all my life in Birmingham and apart from trips to Rhyl or Blackpool, I hadn't been anywhere, let alone abroad. I collected loads of souvenirs and photographs to show the family when I got home. It's strange when I think about it now. We were at war and the future uncertain, but I was collecting souvenirs. The thing was, you didn't think it would be you who got it. On Friday night we all went back to see the Taj Mahal by moonlight. It was brilliant, it looked like a shimmering iceberg, translucent and changing colour depending where the moon was in the sky. It was built with white marble, inside and out and the two tombs of the Shah and Mumtaz Mahal were inlaid with precious jewels in the shape of exotic flowers. Four minarets were positioned at each corner of the courtyard and they allowed us up one of them. There was a spectacular view from the top, you could see everything for miles. We left Agra on Saturday morning and were back in Bareilly by Sunday night. It was so hot in Bareilly. We drank at least twelve pints of lime juice each day, plus loads of tea, but as soon as we drank it, we would sweat it straight out.

A lot of chaps were still getting dysentery through drinking untreated water and careless eating habits. We kept telling them, but it didn't seem to help. Fifty percent of the British troops had dysentery and there was a high incidence of tick typhus; over three thousand cases in one ten week period. One of the most persistent things was skin disease. We all had some form of it and it used to take months to clear it up, but we had to

A visit to the Taj Mahal

A visit to the Taj Mahal

A visit to the deserted City of Fatephur Sikri

live with it unless it got too bad. Many of us suffered through the lack of vitamins and malaria was a constant problem, with very few avoiding it. The army gave us mepacrine, small yellow tablets, but they only held it at bay and had to be taken every day. Eventually, we developed a yellow tinge to our skin as the colour from the tablets was absorbed by our system. As soon as we stopped taking them, a malaria attack would start. It was said that some soldiers deliberately didn't take their mepacrine so they would contract malaria and avoid action. I don't know about that, but the amount of casualties suffering from malaria certainly kept us busy and drastically reduced the number of men available for action.

We were getting a lot of trouble with the Congress Wallahs around this time - Gandhi and his civil disobedience. There was a lot of unrest throughout the country. There had been crop failures and many people were dying of starvation. This caused panic and led to a lot of riots, so our unit was put on full alert. It made me think what was the point in stopping the Japs from taking India, these people were certainly not helping the situation. India wasn't the best place to be at that time, but the choice wasn't ours.

CHAPTER FOUR

We usually stayed in peacetime barracks. The food wasn't too bad. Contractors supplied all the food in India. They were told what was wanted and always managed to get it from somewhere. During the dry season there wasn't a blade of grass anywhere and yet sometimes we had salad for tea. Lettuce, tomatoes, cucumber; a typical salad. It was over a hundred and twenty degrees in the shade at times. We were told to be careful with water, but there never seemed to be a shortage. Yet there was six months without rain and the heat was terrific. Fruit was plentiful, but it was usually rather bland and tasteless. Mangoes were one of my favourites, but they were an acquired taste. Oranges, pineapples and watermelons were also popular and there were also a variety of tropical fruits that we had never heard of before and often wished we hadn't, they gave us the trots. In fact, everything out there gave us the trots and it wasn't always easy to get toilet paper. The main fruit in some areas was pineapple and sacks of them would be delivered. Every day it was pineapples; we got sick of pineapples in the end and yet at home, people never saw one for years. Next to tea, the main drink was lime juice. We could get fresh limes locally and these were nearly always made into lime juice, they were far too sour to eat raw, but these and the other fruits contained many vitamins that were essential in view of the rest of our diet.

There was a small swimming pool at the camp and we were allowed to use it when the officers were not there. I was bathing in there one night and was told to report to the CO's office at once. I didn't have time to change; I had to go there straight away in my swimming trunks. He told me that twelve of us were being posted the next day. He wouldn't tell us where. He just said it was secret and urgent. It was a right rush. We were given a medical, booster inoculations, prepared full kit and were on parade, ready in full marching order by three in the afternoon. It was quite a do. The CO did his inspection and we marched off to the station headed by the band of the Jat Regiment. We didn't know the reason for the pomp and ceremony at the time, but found out afterwards; it was because the CO had received an urgent instruction to send twelve top tradesmen to help with the evacuated casualties from Burma. The CO wanted to uphold the name of the 14th British General Hospital (BGH), so sent eleven first class Nursing Orderlies and me, a first class Operating Theatre Technician. It was late afternoon, about four o'clock, when we got on the train and away we went. We all gave a sigh of relief to get away from the 'army bull'. We didn't know how lucky we were until later. We travelled all that Friday night right through Saturday and arrived at Gaya rest camp at four o'clock on the Sunday afternoon. It was a hell of a journey, we went through Lucknow, Benares, Moghal-Sarai and even crossed over the River Ganges, a very long way from Bareilly.

The trains in India had carriages reserved for British troops with beds that pulled down. Not beds as we knew them, they were just boards and had no padding either. All troops were issued with a type of carpet when travelling. We took it everywhere with us. It was part of our kit and also served as a mattress. The conditions on the train were uncomfortable. The climate was so hot and humid. We left the windows open during the day and that helped, but at night they were shut tight. They had to be. The majority of the Indians travelled on the outside of the coaches, hanging on where they could and would nick anything they could get their hands on if the windows were left open. This made the inside of the coach extremely hot and we got very little sleep. When we stopped at the station, we got water from the engine to make our tea. It tasted horrible but at least the water had been boiled. You couldn't trust the quality of the water from the local stations. You couldn't take the chance. The stations themselves were incredible places. Everybody unrolled a bed and slept on the platform. Mind you, the trains were totally unpredictable. They never arrived on time and were usually several days late. The timetables were just a waste of time. No-one took any real notice of them. Some Indians spent a lifetime on the station, especially the beggars. You could get anything; have a haircut and shave on the platform by the barber wallahs for two pence (2d) and even have your feet and hands manicured. Everything was centred around the railway station and there were always hundreds of people there and a tremendous noise and bustle all the time. It was like a huge bazaar. The charwallahs brewed tea all day and night. The tea urn never seemed to get emptied, just added to. It was kept boiling hot by a charcoal fire attached to the bottom and the tea came out hot, thick brown and very sweet. We still drank it though, we reckoned no germs could live in that. It had to be safe.

Rest camps were set up all over India, Bengal, the Assam and Burma. You would stay there until orders come through to move on. We were at Gaya rest camp and it was hot. We were billeted in tents as usual. We checked in and it was the same old story, no one knew anything about us, so we kept out of the way, had a good clean up, washed our clothes and had a good sleep. We stayed there until the following Thursday and then orders came through for us to immediately proceed to Gauhati in northeast Assam. We moved out in lorries filled with equipment, four at a time, bound for Calcutta. They told us to keep our eyes on the Indian drivers in case they tried to steal or sell the loads to anyone. India was so large that it took days to get from one city to the next; by road it was worse. Once you left the town the roads were just dirt tracks. In the dry season they were rock hard and dusty, whilst in the rainy season they were pure, thick mud and virtually impassable. We arrived in Calcutta at nine o'clock on the Saturday morning completely shattered. We could hardly walk. All of us were covered in thick dust, and you could only see the white of our teeth. I would have given anything for a gallon of cold beer. I could see some on the bar, but it turned out to be a mirage. That's the state we were in.

We checked in at movement control in Calcutta and signed over the equipment and lorries to them and asked where we were to go. The officer knew nothing about us, we weren't expected. He told us to clear off, so we did and went to a local barracks for a wash and brush up and then to the cookhouse for a meal. We pretended we were part of the unit stationed there. It was easy, nobody questioned us, the security wasn't up to much. Then, we had a good look round Calcutta, had a few drinks and at night we went to a Salvation Army hostel. It was only eight annas, (about 4.5p) for bed and breakfast; that suited us. It was quite good, except for all the down and outs. There were all sorts in there, all colours and creeds, an amazing place. I wouldn't have fancied staying there on my own, it looked dodgy. On Sunday morning, we went back to the movement control to see what was happening but no orders had come. We managed to scrounge fifteen rupees off them; we had to, we were flat broke. We used it to go for a meal and then spent the rest of the day strolling around Calcutta again. There was a lot of poverty and unrest at the time because of Gandhi and the starvation riots. It was a rough place and we had to be careful. Some of the dead were left lying in the streets, waiting for members of their own religion to pick them up and take them away. No-one would touch the body of another caste.

We were having a meal in a cafe when the Red Caps burst in. They had been looking all over Calcutta for us and we were piled onto a waiting truck. We went back to movement control and they told us we should have been on a train two days ago and on our way to our destination. They had dropped the clanger, not us. We were on the train by four thirty that afternoon and on our way. It was the Bengal and Assam Railway, a real primitive affair as I remember. They had dirty coaches with hard wooden seats, all bug ridden. It had a top speed of thirty miles per hour. We travelled all-night and reached Amingaon in the late afternoon of the next day. It was a different type of journey this time, the railway went straight through the jungle not barren flatlands. The scenery was fascinating, high trees and thick undergrowth, mainly Bamboo, but dark and foreboding and very humid.

When we got to Amingaon, we boarded a very old paddle steamer, a ferryboat that had been made in Scotland back in 1893; the engine was in really good nick. It was run and maintained by an old Scottish chap who came over with the boat forty-nine years earlier. We travelled all-night and part of the next day up the Brahmaputra River. There was no accommodation for sleeping, we all slept on deck and got bitten to death by flies, millions of them. We couldn't keep them away. Every known and unknown species must have had a taste of me. It was interesting to see all the wild life on the banks of the river, animals, birds, crocodiles, all types of things. I would have loved to get some photographs, but didn't have any film. The river was really wide and full of water snakes and some very peculiar looking fish. Nobody swam in it because it was too fast flowing and dangerous. The noise in the jungle at night was terrific, the frogs never shut up. There were millions of fireflies. They were incredible, you could read by the light of the fireflies. They seemed to light up the whole riverbank - a beautiful sight. Eventually we reached Pandu, a tiny little place, in fact, it was so small it wasn't even marked on the map. We disembarked there and then went by lorry to a clearing about twenty miles east of a place called Gauhati, on the bank of the Brahmaputra River. There, we were put into bashas, small huts made out of bamboo with thatched roofs. These were real basic conditions, no beds of any sort and no lighting either. I had been forewarned in Calcutta and had managed to get a few candles from a bazaar shop. Worst of all, we had no fresh food. We had been living on canned rations since leaving Bareilly and were issued with some tea, condensed milk and sugar. I don't know what we would have done without our tea, it was essential. Everybody seemed to drink it, no matter how bad it tasted. There was another good thing, we could go into the jungle and get some wild bananas. They were real big fat things with big black seeds in them. We were a bit dubious about the fish in the river though, so we tried some on one of our mates who had malaria. We watched him eat it and he survived, so we all had some. It wasn't the best, but it made a change.

We were told the average rainfall of Assam, Bengal and North Burma was over four hundred inches each year, an enormous amount by our standards. It was very hot and humid and nearly always raining and thus, a very steamy atmosphere seemed to prevail all the time. You were never dry there. You went to bed wet, got up wet, stayed wet all day; nothing ever dried, it just went green with mould; even the cigarettes burst open and matches were useless. It was just a waste of time trying to keep anything dry. We had been travelling for over fourteen days and were pleased to reach the rest camp despite the conditions. Our clothes were filthy and our socks even worse, they were vile. We had a good clean up, washed our clothing, wrung them out and put them straight back on. We didn't try to dry them, there was no point. We spent four days there and were issued with some cigarettes and safety matches, for what good they were. None of us had any money and if we had, there was nowhere to spend it. Then, they issued us with jungle green clothing and Australian type bush hats. These were a lot better as the shorts we had were useless in that type of country; we were getting bitten and scratched to pieces. We even wore putties, a type of gaiter, around our ankles because of snakebites or whatever else fancied a nip of you. Shortly after, a Padre came along and we had an outside prayer service. This took us by surprise a bit and made us wonder what was in store. It was quite an anxious time with two hundred men at the camp waiting for transport to various units. This was our first taste of real jungle conditions and it took some getting used to. There was a great sense of comradeship and a fantastic sense of humour. We would have given up without it; some poor sods did. A group of twenty of us were told to report to another camp near Pandu and as an exercise we had to walk the eighteen miles through virgin jungle; our kit went by road, a journey of some fifty miles. They issued us with machetes, a broad bladed, chopping knife and we had to hack our way through the thick bamboo and undergrowth every inch of the way. The jungle was a horrible place; hot, sticky, wet and miserable. When my repatriation papers came through I returned to India the same way I had came three years earlier and was amazed to see places where I had been stationed had vanished. The jungle had completely taken over. When you consider that bamboo can grow several feet in twenty-four hours in some places, you can see why. Incidentally, a General who was allowed back into Burma sixteen years after the war had ended said that it was hard to find any evidence that a war had even taken place in some areas. The tons of damaged equipment that had been left behind had all rusted away and sunk into the swampy jungle floor.

It took us two days to get to the camp and we were totally exhausted when we got there. Our legs were covered in leeches and bamboo thorns and when I took my boots off my socks were saturated in blood, caused by squashed leeches. They must have slipped in through the lace holes. The only way to remove a leech was to put a lighted cigarette end to its backside or wait till it dropped off. You would never try to pull or force it off or it would leave its 'teeth' in your flesh causing an abscess. The camp we landed up at was an Indian rest camp and we joined up with them and had our first hot meal for about a month. It was a curry, hot too, but tasted great. We had some hot sweet tea as well - nectar, the first we had drunk for two days. Eventually we boarded a train to Dimapur. That was the railhead for the area. We took some bananas and pineapples with us and of course, our old friends bully beef and biscuits, not forgetting our precious water bottle. We couldn't cope without that. It took fifteen hours to reach Dimapur and that was as far as you could go by train. After that it was either by lorry, mule or on foot. Those were the only options because the railhead was at the foot of the Naga Hills, a particularly inhospitable terrain. When we got off the train, we checked into 'number three' reinforcement camp, which was, typical of our luck, right smack in the middle of the jungle and, as usual, in utter chaos. Most of these camps had only just started up due to the rapid advance by the Japs and were the only thing the army had organised for the troops to go in or out of Burma, the only other way was through China. Unfortunately, nothing was properly organised, but the American engineers were there with some heavy plant and equipment, pulling up teak trees by their roots and bulldozing the ground flat. It was a fantastic sight to see them working, day and night non-stop and also seeing elephants working for the first time. They were brilliant. We watched in awe as they pulled these huge trees to the sawmills. The men in charge were called mahouts and stayed with their elephants for life, there was an unbreakable bond between them and they understood each other perfectly. They were a pleasure to watch. It was still hot and humid. You sweated like mad, you couldn't help it. The water was so chlorinated it was like drinking pure bleach. We would have done without if there was any other choice, but there wasn't, so that was that.

Then we were posted to Dibrugarh, near the Chinese border and it took just over a day for us to get there by rail. This was a shocking place, more primitive than anywhere we had been. We reported to the camp officer and typically he knew nothing about us. He suggested that we had possibly been sent to join General Stillwell's Chinese army which was trying to contain the Japs in the north east of Burma, but he didn't really know, so we had to remain there until we found out. We spent three days there. It was hopeless. There was no organisation and we had no idea what was happening next. Then, lo and behold, we were told to report back to Dimapur. We couldn't believe it. It seemed such a waste of time and resources and we weren't in the mood for all that travelling again. We looked really rough. We hadn't had a shave for some time, not a haircut for months and we all looked that mucky brown colour that everyone seemed to acquire out there. We could have easily joined one of the local tribes, no problem. When we reached Dimapur, we had a wash and tidy up and even managed to wash our clothes. We should have really washed our clothes daily because of the sweat, but there was no chance of that. Afterwards, we settled down to a meal of corned beef rissoles and baked beans. It tasted great and we washed it down with loads of hot sweet tea. I'm sure the army would have collapsed without tea. You could keep going on tea. It didn't seem to matter about the food so much, but you needed the fluid because of the heat and constant sweating.

We went to see the camp officer to see what was going on and he told us we were soon to be on the move to Kohima. Kohima and Imphal were the last places the Japs needed to capture to make their invasion of India possible. The Allies thought the jungle and terrain of that area was impenetrable and the Japs couldn't attack with sufficient force to penetrate our defences. Kohima itself was a small township, perched on top of a mountain, some five thousand feet above sea level and only a small detachment of troops were employed for its protection, just outside the town at the garrison itself. It was mainly used as a forward supply depot and convalescence centre, plus a rest camp for travelling troops on their way to and from Burma. The terrain surrounding Kohima was all mountains and very thick virgin jungle. The town overlooked the Dimapur to Imphal road, the only road capable of carrying supplies and troops through this area of India into Burma. It was an extremely important strategic place. Should it have been captured, the whole of the 14th Army would have been completely cut off.

We left by truck the next day, thirteen of us with me in charge, to join seven others that had left earlier. We had no map. We just had a rough idea where we were. We didn't really know. The names of places meant nothing. It didn't really matter to us where we were, we just got on with it. I didn't keep my diary up to date either, it was too dangerous, especially if you got caught. Anyway, it was forbidden, so the days just drifted by. They all seemed the same, there was no real pattern, no weekends off, nothing like that at all. We got rationed up so to speak, found our truck and by six in the morning we were on our way to Kohima. The journey was hair raising, right through Nagaland. The road was cut out of the mountainside and just wide enough for one vehicle to pass, with over a thousand-foot drop if you came off the edge of the road. In fact, it was such a vital route, in order to keep the road open, if a truck broke down and it couldn't be repaired quickly, it was pushed over the side. There was no messing about. It had to be done. Things had to be kept moving. We arrived at Kohima at five in the evening and stayed there for three days and then we were told we had to go on to Imphal urgently as soon as any transport was available. We left Kohima mid morning and after another gruelling ride, we arrived at the 51st rest camp at Imphal around about seven in the evening, only to stay overnight before being posted to the 41st Indian General Hospital at Kangletombi, about five miles away. Kanglatongbi, in Naga language means home of the fly and it certainly was, every sort, with the mosquito coming an easy first. They were everywhere. Despite that, as places go, it wasn't bad, a clearing just outside the jungle on the edge of the plain of Imphal. At the back of the hospital lay a range of mountains, part of the Naga and Kachin Ranges. These were very remote areas indeed, almost unchanged for centuries. Over the road was a small REME (Royal Electrical and Mechanical Engineers) camp and not far away was a unit of West Africans, which we used as guides from time to time. They were a real savage lot. One of them died whilst we were there and was given a military funeral with all the pomp and ceremony. This of course cut no ice with them and during the night they dug the body up and did the funeral their way, dancing and chanting, with tom toms banging all night. You felt you were in the middle of an African jungle.

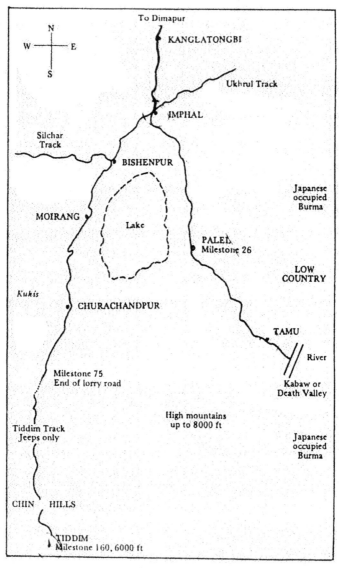

The Tiddim Track

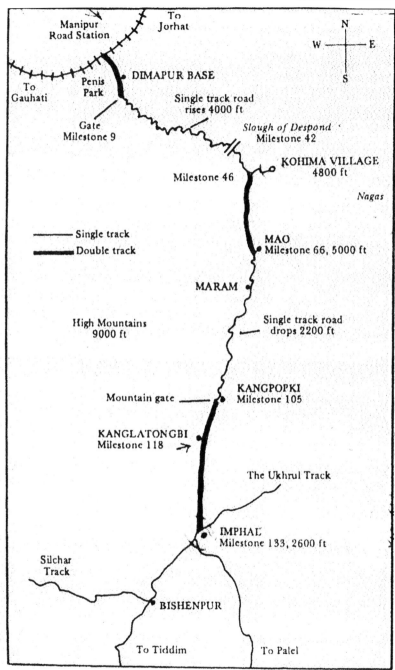

The Dimapur – Imphal Road

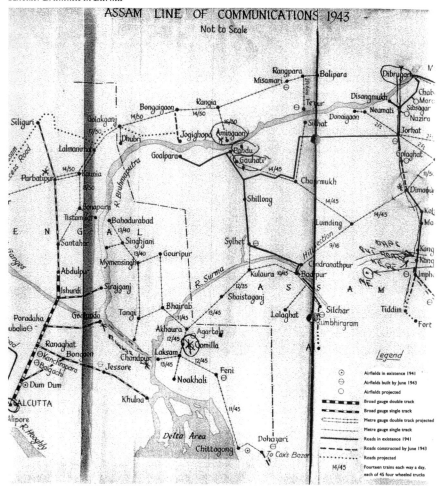

It had been thirty-eight days since we had left Bareilly and we had certainly clocked up some mileage. When our new CO interviewed us, he said we should have been flown in from Calcutta, as it was a top priority posting from General Headquarters (GHQ) in Delhi. That didn't make us feel any better. All that travelling takes it out of you. The reason we should have been flown directly to Imphal was that the 41st IGH (Indian General Hospital) was rapidly admitting more and more British troops and the staff that were already there couldn't cope. Originally, it had been built for two hundred and fifty patients, but when we arrived it had well over a thousand. They were all mixed races and in terrible shape. The conditions within the hospital itself were also suffering due the number of casualties. The Area Commander had instructed GHQ at Delhi to send a contingent of British medics urgently. When the twenty of us arrived, he came to see us and wanted to know why it took so long to get there and where the hell we had been. I told him about all the delays and cock-ups we had come up against and he realised it wasn't our fault. He was a General and wasn't amused. He said he would have a few words with various people and straighten a few things out when he got in touch with Movement Control in Delhi. He explained what was going on at the hospital and told us a British Colonel, plus a surgeon Lt Colonel and four British Medical Officers would be taking over control of the hospital, assisted by the eight Indian doctors already there. Those that had just arrived were all NO (Nursing Orderly) Class 1, plus me, an Operating Assistant Class 1. The General was quite impressed. He told us to commence at once and see if we could get some order out of the chaos. We were to report to him if we had any trouble from anyone and he would sort it out. You see, we had some mixed race and different castes amongst the orderlies. They were quite good but needed direction and it was essential to the operation of the hospital that we got them up to speed without delay. The main problem was the language. There are so many different dialects of the Indian language that often, one Indian didn't always know what the other was on about. It made life very complicated, but fortunately most of them could speak a certain amount of pidgin English, which was good really. We only knew a limited amount of Hindi and this coupled with a lot of arm waving allowed us to communicate with each other. It was difficult, but after some trial and error, we got what we wanted. The hospital wards were bashas made out of bamboo and thatch. They weren't too bad, but were not adequate for the number of patients that started to pour in. It had originally been set up when things were quieter, but now that the retreat from Burma was taking place, things altered on a daily basis and nearly always for the worst. On one occasion we nearly lost the whole hospital after a fire had started. Some Nagas were 'slashing and burning' the undergrowth so they could cultivate the land. Unfortunately, some embers caught one of the bashas and in no time at all the fire spread to some of others. We lost about a third of the hospital in total, including part of the quartermaster's stores. We managed to get it under control and luckily no-one was hurt. The damage was soon put right. Coolies rebuilt the burnt bashas within a few days. The hospital was soon fully operational again and the normal daily chaos prevailed. To add to the confusion, the monsoon started once again, non-stop rain day and night for weeks on end. We were under canvas as usual and the weather and the insects made it a very miserable time. There were so many flies and creepy-crawlies. We always had to sleep under our mosquito nets.

There were no amenities at all. The first thing we did was to ask for a British cook and to our surprise, we got one. He was brilliant. He had to be with us lot. He could cook corned beef fifty different ways, but it beat him when we started getting corned mutton. It was disgusting and came out of the tin in a thick runny mass. There was no way you could eat it. It looked revolting and smelt awful so, straight in the bin it went. We seldom had fresh bread either, it was nearly always dry biscuits or the Indian type flat pieces of bread the locals had, called chapattis. They were quite nice. When we had settled in awhile, we used to go out and shoot pigeons or sometimes a wild pig for a change of menu. We would also barter salt with the Nagas, in exchange for some fresh eggs and chickens. We seemed to adapt to most situations. It was no good standing there saying what shall we do about this or that, you just did it. One example of this was that we had nowhere to eat, so we built a mess room ourselves; a real posh job as well. We made it out of bamboo and trunks of trees; it was that good even the officers asked if they could use it.

We all worked as a team, the officers and men alike. There was no 'army bull' of any sort, it wouldn't have worked otherwise. The British other ranks virtually ran the hospital. They were fully qualified and very dedicated too and rather than sit in their tents when off duty, they would be on the wards working. They were incredible. We had a lot of casualties coming in from the retreating troops in Burma with all sorts of terrible injuries, plus hundreds of malaria, typhus and dysentery cases. I had worked in the operating theatre since I arrived and also did most of the surgical dressings on the wards. It really kept me busy and like the others there was no such thing as time off. We were glad to hear that six British sisters had arrived, thinking that would ease the pressure we were under, but it didn't work out that way. They couldn't cope with the amount of work. The CO put them in charge of the officers' wards. As it happened, that did help because some of the old pre-war British officers were a right pain and expected to be waited on hand and foot. Of course, that didn't work with us. They were given the same treatment as the others and they didn't like it, but when the sisters came, we left it to them to sort out.

The engineers built a large concrete water storage tank on the side of the hill near the hospital, about thirty by twenty feet and six feet deep and they allowed us to swim in it. It became the highlight of our lives, there wasn't much else to do and we used to go there as often as possible. We went in rain or shine. It was very refreshing after being in the heat and the water was always warm. Also, we played football against other local units when possible, but the pitch was never up to much, it was like playing in a swamp. We nearly always lost, we just didn't have the time to practice and the sweat just poured out of us. Frankly, I would have rather spent my time off in the swimming tank, that was much more fun. We only ever wore shorts and a hat during the day, but at night, we wore a shirt and trousers because of the mosquitoes. My skin had by now, turned real deep brown and had the texture of leather because of the climate. All of us had long hair and beards; it seemed to suit the environment we were in. None of us were bothered with parades, roll calls and drills. That's not to say we were not disciplined, we were. The CO just went along with what we did. He relied on us and he knew we wouldn't let him down anyway

The monsoons prevailed for eight months of the year. In August, it rained every day and night non-stop, the ground just became a sea of mud and we were constantly wet. We were issued with special monsoon capes, but couldn't wear them for long. They made us sweat too much. We were at the bottom of a mountain that we called Mountbatten Peak and for weeks we could never see the top, it was always covered in cloud. We were on fairly high ground but it was like being under a waterfall when the worst rains came. We dug deep trenches round the tents to try to divert the water, but it still ran through the hospital like a river. It rained so heavily that you couldn't see through it at times. All the wards leaked. The poor patients had to sleep with ground sheets over them to try to keep dry. It was a dreadful situation, but everyone accepted it. There was no alternative. It could have been worse. I have seen whole buildings washed away during the monsoon when a local river changed its course.

Our tents were in a mess. The floor was covered with thick mud and we had very little room with six men to a tent. One tiny oil lamp was hung in the middle to give us a bit of light. It attracted hundreds of flies. They formed a huge funnel from the floor to the lamp, but at least it kept them off us. Our beds were called charpoys and made of bamboo, criss-crossed with rope then covered with a mattress filled with straw, the whole structure being about eighteen inches off the floor. On each corner was

Monsoon clouds forming over the Imphal Plains

a pole on which we hung our mosquito nets. The nets were really vital and you had to be careful how you put them on. If one mosquito got under the net, the noise it made could keep you awake all night. You would hear it whining around you and when you couldn't hear it, you knew it had landed and was stinging you. Then you knew it was almost guaranteed you would get malaria. After a long spell on duty, I returned to my tent in the early hours one morning and fell straight into my bed. I couldn't see much and pulled the mosquito net down before going to sleep. Suddenly, something cold and wet fell onto my face and was writhing about. I thought it must be a snake. I instantly froze and lay perfectly still, hardly daring to breathe. I tried to communicate as best I could with my mate in the next bed, by talking through my teeth. Thankfully he got the message and with the aid of what little light there was from the Tilly lamp, he gently lifted the net, his revolver at the ready to blow the thing off my face. I didn't fancy that either, he wasn't that good a shot. The moment of truth arrived and he burst out laughing. He leant forward and picked the thing off my face. It was a huge frog. It was big as well, it must have weighed nearly two pounds. The whole experience left me shattered. It frightened me to death. We had loads of these type of creatures and snakes about especially during the monsoon. Cobras and kraits where the worst, very poisonous indeed. During the day, my mate Bill was having a snooze before going on night duty. He slept completely naked because of the heat. We all did. I happened to look down by his bed and saw something move. It was a krait snake gliding towards his foot. Without hesitation, I grabbed my kukri and chopped it to bits. I woke up Bill to tell him, but only got a load of verbal abuse for spoiling his nap. I even had to clear the mess up myself.

I managed to get fifty rupees pay, the first money I had received for two months. They also told me I was one hundred and fifty rupees in credit since we hadn't been paid for such a long time. It didn't really matter, there wasn't a lot to spend your money on; no shops or naafi out there. I did manage to borrow a jeep that the RE's (Royal Engineers) had acquired, made up from bits and pieces of wrecked vehicles they had come across and so, four of us went into Imphal. I drove and it was a pretty hair raising journey on those roads, especially with my driving. There was not much to do when we got there, but we did manage to get some pipe tobacco and cigars, which was quite interesting. They hand rolled the cigars while you waited, nice and fresh and about a foot long. The pipe tobacco looked like a big, old Christmas pudding and they just tore a lump off and wrapped it up in a leaf for us. We put it in a tin when we got back and soaked it in rum. It smoked marvellous. We joked that it killed all the flies for miles around. We also got a few odds and ends from the local bazaar, nothing fancy, just cheap rubbish really, but it was nice to do a bit of shopping. Imphal was only a small place then and seemed quite insignificant, but we had no idea how important it would become.

In September, we moved from the tents into bashas. They were not much better than the tents, but there was more room to move about. The rain still let in, but we stuck our monsoon capes on top of the mosquito nets and that helped to keep the beds a little drier. We hadn't received any mail since June. There had been landslides on the mountain roads between Kohima to Imphal and nothing could get through except the essential stuff and that came by air. We were supposed to get three bottles of beer a month and a ration issue of cigarettes, but none arrived, so I smoked the local Burmese cheroots or my pipe. We had a few Anglo-Indian girls working on the Indian wards. They weren't too bad and we were glad of the help. One of them died, poor thing. She had a severe lung infection. They gave her a military funeral at Imphal, I was one of the bearers, not a pleasant task. When someone dies, they have to be buried the next day because of the heat and it is usual to pack the body with ice to slow down the decomposition. Well, this began to melt and started running down my neck as I was carrying the coffin.

We were always very busy in the hospital and by now the convoys were arriving on a daily basis, bringing casualties from the troops fighting in central Burma. They were always in a bad state by the time they reached us. I used to wonder how they survived the journey. We had a group of Scottish troops, a right rough lot, as tough as hell, who had fought all the way from Singapore, right across Thailand and Burma. They were suffering from everything, including venereal disease and they were completely exhausted. They couldn't care less for anyone or anything and as far as they were concerned the rules didn't apply to them. A group of them were playing cards one night and one of them cheated, so he was shot dead. The next night one of them was stabbed to death in a brawl after drinking some of the local jungle juice, right potent stuff. A court martial took place, but no one owned up or said who the culprits were. That's how they were. It was just an accepted way of life to them. They had suffered terrible hardships, it must have been survival of the fittest in the shocking conditions that they encountered and more than seventy five percent of them had been killed. Anyway, they were all sent down the line to India. We were glad to get rid of them. They were too explosive for us and we had enough to do without worrying about them.

Men were dying at the rate of about five a night in the Indian section of the hospital. It used to be a lot more, but since we took over, we managed to get the figure down to single numbers. The biggest problem was still the language. We had to rely on the Indian orderlies to sort out the food and the various castes. We didn't have the time. We tried to send the worst cases, both British and Indian, down the line to hospital in Calcutta or to my old unit, the 14th BGH at Bareilly, but it was a hell of a long way by road and train. It was touch and go whether some of them would make it. So, we tried to fly them out but there wasn't that many spare planes and anyway they were busy elsewhere. We kept trying though, but in the meantime, we just carried on and hoped for the best. Outside, it continued raining and everything was covered in a sea of mud and the smell that went with it. This was quite a depressing time for us. We found it hard to cope and the weather didn't help. Then in September, we were told Italy had surrendered, so to celebrate we were given a bottle of rum, one between four of us. It was made in India but quite good really and gave us a bit of a lift. We certainly needed one. It was funny really; we seemed to be able to get rum from time to time, but nothing else; no beer or other spirits, just the usual, tea and lime juice.

Shortly after, it was my mate, Reg Hiley's birthday. He got some rum from somewhere, so we all had a drink to celebrate. He mixed his with some of the local fermented rice water and wandered off somewhere. He was missing for two days, so we had to send out a search party. We eventually found him after a long search. He was in a bamboo thicket about two miles away and still drunk. We were warned about the rice water, it was very dangerous. The locals fermented it in a hollow section of bamboo and it turned out real rough stuff. Sometimes they distilled it and this made it a really potent brew. The locals reckoned if you drunk too much it would send you blind. I don't know about that, but Reg was in a right state when we found him. It took him days to recover. About two o'clock one morning, poor Reg was sleeping off the effects of the local brew, when suddenly, there was a tremendous crash. It was pitch black, raining and Reg came running out of his basha shouting his head off. We thought the Japs had broken through. We were about to get ready for action, when it went all quiet again. I lit a couple of oil lamps and the reason for the commotion was revealed. Above Reg's bed was the head of a water buffalo, a real ugly, big thing with huge horns. The poor thing had been grazing outside the basha and in the darkness butted its head through the flimsy wall. Well, Reg hadn't pulled his mosquito net down and awoke to be greeted by this creature and a blast of its not so pleasant breath. Obviously in the darkness he didn't hang about. We found him though. He was all right and took time out to blame the whole episode on us for some reason only known to himself. Despite the odd lighter moments, things were pretty fraught. There was still no mail and it was the 18th October when I received my next letter from home; it had been posted on the 9th July. No wonder we called ourselves the forgotten army. It was the same with equipment and supplies, they were always late or short. We understood that Europe must come first, but things were getting desperate out there. We needed all the help we could get.

A Devon Regiment came down from Tamu. They had been evacuated because nearly all of them were down with tick typhus. Apparently, they caught it by sleeping in flea infested bashas and had walked about sixty miles to get to us. They were in a terrible state, those that made it. Quite a lot of them had died on the way. We also had an influx of troops from other regiments stationed at Palel suffering with typhus and glandular fever. Soon the hospital was stretched to full capacity, everyone working flat out in primitive conditions, with very little essential medi-

Left to Right - Bill Asprey, Reg Hiley, Len Thornton

cines to do the job in hand. We asked for an air supply drop, but they said it would take over a week to get it because of other priorities. Our CO managed to get a DC3 cargo plane allocated to us, based at Imphal, so this other chap and myself flew over the mountains to Comilla, the nearest hospital to us at the time, to get some emergency supplies. We got a little but nowhere near enough. We flew out one day and came back the next. That was really quick because by road it would have taken two weeks or more. We were just finishing unloading the plane, sweating and cursing as usual, when suddenly out of nowhere, the Japs attacked with eighteen aircraft dropping bombs all around us. The only planes we had at that time were six ancient Buffaloes and they flew off when the Jap Zeros came in. They were no match for them. We had no anti aircraft guns and so we had to wait until they cleared off and hope for the best. They did a lot of damage and quite a lot of troops were injured or killed, including ten British soldiers who were awaiting repatriation home because of ill health. A bomb dropped right in the middle of their tent. Some of our chaps were sent down to sort things out. It was awful. My mate Bill and I took refuge underneath the truck we were loading, it was no good trying to run anywhere, the Japs machine-gunned anything that moved. It all happened so quickly. When you saw the bombs dropping, it seemed that each one was aimed directly at you. This was the first time Imphal had been attacked by planes and it caused a lot of concern as it meant the Japs had established forward air bases and could attack at will. Things didn't look good at all. In fact it was just a foretaste of things to come. Eventually, we got back to the hospital with the supplies and, of course, got the usual cracks from our mates such as: where had we been; where did we get the brown trousers from, and more of the same. We didn't care though; we were just glad to get out.

I developed a huge abscess on my left thigh, caused by a sliver of bamboo. The pain was awful. I could hardly walk. I dosed myself up with sulphanilamide tablets and after eight days of sheer agony it started to clear up. I wasn't the only one, all the lads seem to suffer from boils and septic sores at one time or another, it seemed to be the norm out there. We had two special cases arrive in from a mule company; one British Officer and an Indian sepoy, both had haemoragic smallpox, deadly and very infectious, the worst type possible. They had to be isolated from the rest and yours truly was asked to take charge of them. Apparently, they looked into my records and found I was immune to smallpox, plus I was single, so that made me a natural choice. The CO had a word with me and said that on no account were they to leave the hut they were in. He also told us that there was no cure to this particular strain of the disease and that they would be dead in forty-eight hours. I was issued with a revolver and some bullets and told if things got awkward and the patients went berserk, "I knew what to do". It was terrible to see this type of smallpox. They just lay there and died within forty-eight hours, just as the CO had said. There was nothing we could do, only make them as comfortable as possible. The hut we had was about fifty yards away from the smallpox hut and when we went to look at the patients we wore a huge white gown which just had slits for our eyes, a pair of wellington boots, rubber gloves and a mouth mask. There was a tin bath full of disinfectant in which we stood when we came out of the hut. We also washed our gloves and hands in it. We took every precaution. We couldn't risk any further infection. Our food and supplies were left in a tent about quarter of a mile from where we were, the isolation hut being about a mile from the hospital itself and no one was allowed near us. No one wanted to anyway. I reported that the patients had died and awaited instructions as to what I was to do next. Eventually the orders came for me to set fire to everything, including our hut. A load of stuff was left for us to carry out the necessary tasks, cans of petrol and two small tents, one for the sepoy and the other for myself, plus some clothing. In fact, everything we needed for the two weeks isolation required before we could go back to our quarters, including a tin bath and gallons of disinfectant. They had to be sure there was no chance of further infection. We could get plenty of water, that was never a problem, it never stopped raining. If we needed it for drinking we boiled it on a little Primus stove we had been given. It was all very primitive. We were allowed extra rations. It was an army rule that anyone looking after infectious cases had the best food available. The CO did us proud, he even sent us some bottles of beer and two bottles of rum. We set fire to the huts, clothes, equipment, everything. We couldn't risk the chance of the disease spreading. Afterwards we had a disinfectant bath all over, then went naked to our new clothes which had been left some distance away. The only things I kept from our stay were the revolver and bullets that I had dipped in disinfectant, just in case. The two weeks went slowly. We kept ourselves busy and went on treks into the jungle away from the hospital. We saw a lot of wild life, all sorts really. I would have given anything for a camera. I spent a lot of time shooting at rats and got quite good at it by the end. The CO must have heard me and sent a message to see if I was running my own private war. That made me smile a bit. At last, we were told we could return to our quarters and were medically examined and given blood tests to make sure we were clear. It all seemed to be okay and we were told we could return, but first, we had to set fire to our tents, clothes and all the other stuff we had been using. Then we had yet another bath in disinfectant, put on our new uniforms and were finally allowed back to our quarters and mates. Some of the lads kept their distance for a time, just to make sure.

An incident happened while we were looking after the smallpox cases that could have been very serious indeed. It could have allowed the disease to spread. The Nagas were headhunters and lived in the mountains at the back of the hospital. Several of them came down a path very near to where we were, just as we were going across to see the patients. It was early morning but still quite dark and the sight of us, dressed from head to foot in our white gowns must have given them quite a shock, but instead of running away they stood their ground, with their spears raised ready to attack. That really took the smile off our faces. The sepoy with me fortunately knew a few words of Naga and he shouted to them in their language. Much to our relief they went away and left us to it. We wouldn't have had a chance had they attacked, they were very fierce people, afraid of nothing. In 1998 I noticed a letter in the 'Dekho', the Burma Star Association magazine, requesting information about the very same officer that had died, nearly fifty-five years after the event. It was from one of his family. I didn't know what to do at first, but in the end I wrote and told them what I knew. I had to. I think they had a right to know and hoped it helped them get over their loss.

It was back to the grind again. I took over full control of the operating theatre, the sergeant who had been in control during my absence had flaked out. He hadn't been well for some time and was sent back to India. He was a smashing chap and taught me a lot when I first got to Imphal. I was next in line for promotion to full corporal and then later to sergeant. We were still working flat out at the hospital. We didn't stop. The Japs were dropping bombs daily and there were air raids at all times. This made us a bit anxious at first, but we got used to it. We acquired a 'Bofors' anti aircraft gun. I know it doesn't sound a lot, but it knocked out six Japs in one go. They came over in line as usual, but didn't know about the gun. They used to come in very low to pick out their targets, but this time they were shot down. They were much more careful after that. On that occasion the debris from the bombers did more damage than the bombs. One of the engines fell straight through the cookhouse. It was quite funny really. We had been joking with the cook that someone would get him one day because of the food. He swore blind that we had organised it.

Another humorous incident involved the matron and it took place at the hospital before the female staff were evacuated. Each week the matron paid a visit round the wards but, because of the conditions we worked under, nothing much was said. She was quite a large person and a bit of a dragon really. This surfaced when we were told that a Lord and Lady Mountbatten were going to visit the hospital. At first we were told that the visit was a week away, but in typical army style, they got it wrong; it was the next day. Well, she went into a right panic, so much so that her Scottish accent became incoherent and nobody could understand what she was on about. We weren't so bad, but the poor Indian orderlies didn't have a clue. We cleaned up as best we could, but the pools of water that we had cleared away were starting to form again, due to the continuous rain and, because we had removed the ground sheets from over the mosquito nets, the patients were getting wet. Of course, they were far from happy and threatened to play up during the visit and complain about the food and conditions. They didn't care, they had done their bit. We pacified them by promising extra portions when they had gone. Anyway, the fateful morning came and our twenty British lads had done the best they could. We even had a wash and shave. The wards were quite reasonable, but between each ward the ground was flooded and to get from basha to basha we used duck boards (made of wooden slats). Usually we never bothered and just waded across the water. We were always soaking wet as it was so it didn't make a lot of difference to us. When the time came, there was the Matron in full regalia, the Queen Alexandra Imperial Military nursing outfit, with the swan like head-dress, red uniform, black cape round her shoulders, and black high-heeled shoes. Everybody looked in awe, a remarkable sight by any standard, especially in those conditions. Lord and Lady Mountbatten were dressed in light-weight khaki battle dress and wore stout brogue shoes and they went from bed to bed with the usual patter. The visit to the first ward went well and the visitors crossed over to the next ward via the duck boards with much care, having the right shoes on helped, but the Matron took one step forward on to the board and fell straight into the pool of muddy water. Eventually she surfaced like a hippo having a mud bath. A group of officers helped her out of the water and off she went and unbelievably had a quick shower, under a bucket with holes in, put on her best khaki uniform and caught up with the visiting group at the last ward. She was tough, she had to be, but after walking out of the last ward she did exactly the same again. She didn't pay us a visit for a week after that and then we heard she had been posted elsewhere. It was a shame really but she couldn't have faced us. We were a rotten shower and she knew it. She did send us a note though, saying thanks for all we had done during her stay at the hospital, but she ended it with a row of question marks. So she did have a sense of humour after all.

CHAPTER FIVE

Things were going from bad to worse. The Japs advanced. Christmas 1943 was just another working day, no booze, no cigarettes, no mail - nothing and it poured down with rain. I had lost track of dates and days. I started my diary again but didn't keep it going. The time ahead looked bleak. We treated each day as it came and accepted what it brought. The British soldier has the knack of making the best of things and there was always one of us cracking a joke or bringing some humour to the worst of situations.

Every now and then the operating theatre ran out of supplies and a few of us would have to fly to somewhere or other to try and scrounge replacements. We flew to Chittagong, Dacca, Calcutta and Comilla to name a few and we would take a letter signed by the General in charge of medical services to prioritise our needs. It worked wonders. We would fly on a DC3 cargo plane. It was great. The pilot enjoyed it too. We all got along very well. We used to bring booze back and we had a shopping list for the officers and our mates that seemed to get longer every trip. But it all came to an end. We were told to make a list of the supplies we required and they would be air dropped.

When they came to Imphal from Northern China, we used to get the American Pilots to swap their tins of spam for our tins of corned beef; they loved it and the spam made a change for us. To supplement our rations we used to barter with the locals. Sometimes we could get a few eggs or a chicken. The local REME unit would go on a pigeon shoot and always bring us some. The Cook used to dress and serve them like chickens. They were very tasty. It was amazing what the chaps would do for food and what the cooks could do with it. One chap came in with a wild boar he had shot. Snakes were also a delicacy with the native troops, not that I fancied them.

We would get a lull in the theatre now and again, so a couple of us used to amble across to the airstrip and go out on the supply drops to other areas. They used to ask for volunteers and we thought it would make a change. It was a bit hair raising but it was different and we liked it. They used to tie ropes around us to keep us in the plane and when the drop area was reached the doors were opened and we would push the supplies out; some with parachutes, some without, depending what was in them. There was always the threat that we could be attacked by the Jap Zeros (planes) or crash, but we tried not to think of that because if that happened we wouldn't have stood a chance, not in that thick jungle, hundreds of miles of it occupied by the Japs. The Japs were still advancing across Burma at an alarming rate and although the British army fought a rear guard action, they were withdrawing all the time. As they retreated they blew up or destroyed the oil fields, railways, ruby mines and bridges; anything that might be useful to the Japs. The amount of casualties was increasing all the time. In the end we had to give up our huts to the patients. It was back to tents for us. We didn't mind that much. Their need was greater than ours. The patients now numbered over two thousand and were of mixed nationalities. To make things worse, all the female staff were sent back to India. We couldn't run the risk of them being captured by the Japs who were getting closer each day.

My old unit, the 14th British General Hospital (BGH) was in transit from India to Imphal. Their advance party came to our hospital and took responsibility for five hundred of the beds to help relieve the pressure on us and to prepare to take over the rest of the hospital when their unit finally arrived. Some of our chaps were being moved on. In fact ten of the original gang of twenty, including me, had been detailed to go to Tiddim and help with the casualties, where the Japs were trying to break through to advance and capture Imphal. Four of us set up an advanced dressing station just behind the front line and prepared to take in the wounded. There was a lot of close fighting. Casualties were coming in all the time. We would patch them up the best we could and then get a truck or ambulance to take them to the base hospital at Imphal. It was a very slow process because of the state of the roads. They were nothing like we know them, just narrow tracks and since it was nearly always raining you can imagine their condition and the condition of the troops when they finally reached safety. It was such a very long journey and in some parts they had to use mules and jeeps to get through where the

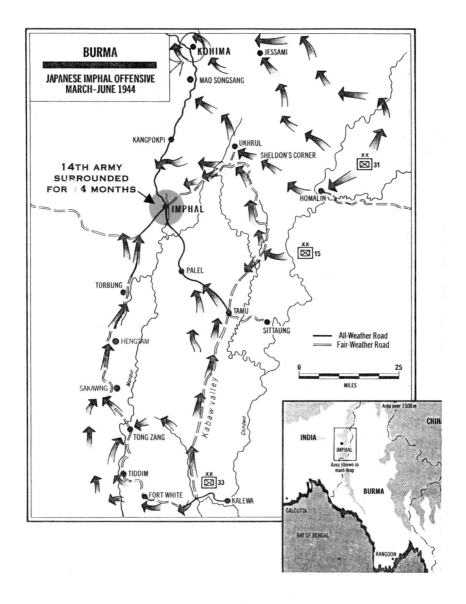

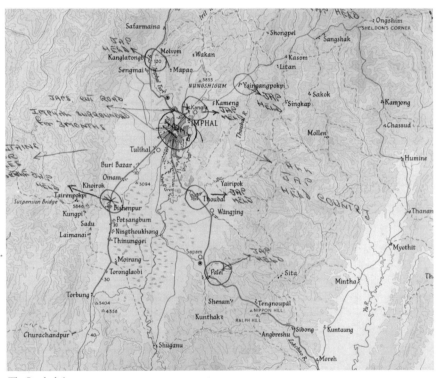

The Imphal Area

lorries and ambulances couldn't make it.

Things were getting very serious at the front and because of the atroci-
ties that the Japs had carried out elsewhere, we kept some weapons by us
that we had acquired from past casualties. A Jap patrol broke into our
first aid area and a hell of a battle raged. It was the first action I had seen.
I had a Sten machine gun and a revolver with me at the time. Suddenly,
a Jap officer came charging at me with his sword waving above his head.
It seemed so unreal, almost as if in slow motion. I stood there frozen. It
was as though I was watching it all from the outside. Fortunately, it only
lasted a few seconds then reaction set in. I squeezed the trigger on my
Sten gun and fired at him. He just came on. I couldn't understand it; I
thought I must be missing him or firing blanks. His face had a terrifying
look on it and he came closer and closer. I couldn't move, I was riveted
to the spot. I suppose it was fear. Then, he gradually fell to the ground
and his sword came to rest on the toe of my boot. At that moment I
realised I had run out of bullets on both weapons so I hid under a truck
where a mate of mine was taking cover. Eventually, the Japs were driven
off and I shouted to my mate to get moving, but he was dead. A bullet
had hit him in the head. He was only a foot from me. That spooked me;
him getting hit so close by. It could have easily been me. It made me
wonder who would be next. Officially I should have left him there, but I
couldn't. I picked him up, put him in a jeep along with some of the
other casualties and made my way back to our unit at Imphal. When I
finally reached our hospital (the 41st IGH at Kanglatongbi) I reported
to the CO what had happened. Afterwards he told me to go to the operating theatre and get my face attended to. It was only then that I realised
that the left-hand side of my face was covered in blood. I went to my
surgeon and he jokingly said I was supposed to treat the patients, not get
hit myself. Anyway, he had a probe round and took out a two-inch piece
of shrapnel from my left eyebrow. It was quite a gash really, another half
inch and I would have lost my eye. The funny thing about it was that I
felt no pain at the time. It was a day later when the pain set in and then
I knew about it. I picked up the Japanese officer's sword, I hadn't got
time to pick up the scabbard. It was attached to him by a thick leather
belt. I managed to get it back to my tent and was going to keep it as a
souvenir but somehow the Colonel got to know about it and he said it
had to be handed in to Intelligence department because the officer's
name was on it. When they had finished with it, he said I would get it
back. Of course, I never saw it again, I reckon the Colonel kept it. I

remember talking to a fellow at a reunion dinner some years ago. He recalled the incident. In fact he was the Sergeant in charge of a platoon looking for that same Jap patrol. He didn't realise any British Troops were on the hill because it was actually in Jap territory, so was our dressing station. Of course we didn't know that at the time and when he heard us firing his platoon charged up the hill and smashed into the Japs killing over seventy of them. The Japs thought we were the patrol they had been looking for and so charged us; all four of us. If the platoon had not arrived, we would have certainly been killed.

We were told to pack everything up and get ready to move to another area. The 14th BGH was going to completely take over. Because our hospital was not up to the standard they wanted they were building a new one about five miles away. On March 16th panic set in. We got new orders to open up again. The Japs were too close and the 14th BGH was to move out of the area with all their equipment, as soon as possible. It was much more up to date than ours and needed to be kept out of Jap hands. That dropped us right in it. Everybody was working flat out trying to get all the equipment back in. We had to look after two thousand patients at the same time. It was a right cock up and the physical effort required to sort it out was enormous, but we did it. What we didn't know was that all the troops had been ordered to withdraw towards Imphal and make up a 'defensive box', whereby troops would withdraw to a designated area and reform, with supplies being brought in by air. We were bombed at least twice a day and the Japs were going berserk. Nothing seemed to stop them.

We had got the hospital into some sort of running order again, when the order came through from Headquarters to evacuate the hospital and patients at once. You can imagine how we felt about that after what we had been through. We couldn't believe it. The CO told us we had less than two days to get out, the Japs were so close. We went straight into action and immediately sent all the walking wounded down to Kohima on any type of transport we could lay our hands on. Then, we sent all the stretcher cases down to the airstrip on anything that would carry them, including the local bullock carts. As we demobilised it was more like a refugee camp than a hospital. Every plane, bombers, fighters, cargo, transport, anything that flew was filled with the wounded and then they were flown over the mountains to Comilla. It was only a small airstrip, so we had to load the wounded onto the planes quickly as other aircraft were arriving and we didn't have much time. It took about twenty minutes to load each one. We couldn't have taken longer. Inside it was so hot, the aircraft was like a sauna while stationary. As soon as they were full, they took off to their destination. They didn't hang around. When they got there, the planes were unloaded and would fly straight back. This continued until every patient had been evacuated. It is difficult to comprehend how we did it. There were only six officers, twenty British other ranks plus the Indian lads to move over two thousand patients to safety. It was worse at night. There were no lights. It was pitch black and raining, but we carried on. I had not taken my boots off for more than a week and my feet were on fire. They were red raw. My socks and boots were full of blood from more squashed leeches. You must appreciate that at that time life was very basic; there was simply not enough hours in the day, no time for niceties. I couldn't remember eating much, there wasn't much around anyway and we didn't get much sleep either and that affected us all, but we did manage to get some mugs of hot, very sweet, tea. That kept us going.

The 14th BGH had by this time abandoned the new hospital and were going in convoy to the railhead at Dimapur with all their equipment. It was a journey of one hundred and sixty miles over the mountain roads and these were really just paths cut out of the rock. The Japs ambushed the last three lorries and some of the chaps I had known from my Oxford days were killed. When they reached Dimapur they were all sent to infantry units to defend the place. You see, Dimapur was on the Japanese hit list. It was important for them to take the railhead as it would give them a direct route through India and also cut off the supply route into Burma. If that happened the 14th Army would be cut off and annihilated or taken prisoner. The Japs didn't respect prisoners; they considered them cowards, feeling that a man should die in battle rather than be captured. They didn't respect anything really and although incredibly brave, they were very barbaric and would torture and kill anyone, women and children included if it suited their cause. Even the RAMC were armed because the Japs didn't recognise the Red Cross Code.

By the time we had evacuated everyone from our hospital it was late Friday/early Saturday morning 31st March 1944. The Colonel called us together. He told us that the Japanese had cut the road from Imphal to Kohima. Not only that, they had cut all other routes and we were totally surrounded. The Japs had surprised an Engineers camp during the night, killed all the troops and set up a roadblock on the only road between Imphal and Kohima. This happened just an hour after we had finished the patient evacuation. Had they been caught, they would have been killed. The Japs didn't take prisoners at that time. That came as a hell of a shock; we didn't know what was going to happen next. We knew the Japs were in the area but didn't know exactly where. We soon found out. They were less than a quarter of a mile away. Some Gurkhas had been rushed up to contain them and all hell broke loose; machine gun, rifle and mortar fire. It was non-stop and we were right in the middle of it. The Japs used a lot of two-inch mortars and they were really raining down all over the place. They were full of large ball bearings, which went everywhere and caused a lot of injuries. We joined the Gurkhas in some trenches they had quickly dug about two hundred yards away and just pointed our weapons and fired. We couldn't see anyone, it was pitch black and raining and the only thing we could see was by the light of the enemy gunfire. Then some more troops arrived. A brigadier saw our CO with us in the trenches and told him to get us out and make our way to Imphal where an emergency hospital was being flown in. This was really crucial because in the chaos, the medical treatment for the wounded was virtually non existent. Sixteen of our lads had got stuck back at the airstrip where they had been organising the evacuation and set up a casualty post nearby. Fortunately most of the Medical Officers were there, otherwise there would not have been any help for the new casualties of which there were many. At this time, all troops had withdrawn to Imphal and the whole area had become a defended box. This fortunately included the airstrip that had to be kept open; it was our lifeline for everything. The airstrip itself was only small, just large enough for a few Hurricanes and DC3 supply planes, plus a few Mitchell, medium sized, bombers. The whole area was about five miles square and continually shrinking under the Jap attacks. To help conserve supplies, all the troops that were not required and as many casualties as possible were flown out. Then, the serious side started, getting in supplies, ammunition and all the other essential stuff and consolidating what we had actually got. On the perimeter of the 'box' fierce fighting was going on all the time, but the 14th army were holding their positions - just.

We didn't really know what to expect next. There were just the four of us and we were all armed to the teeth. I had a Thompson machine gun, an American gangster type, the other lads had Sten guns. We all had revolvers, grenades and knives. We thought if this was it, we could at least put up some resistance and have a go. So, we started off over the hills and headed towards the defensive box at Imphal, some miles away.

We didn't really need a map, we could tell where it was by the sound of gunfire and the flashes in the sky. On the way out of the hospital site we broke into the Red Cross stores and took some tins of marmite and some tins of fruit. We didn't want the fruit in the tins, we just wanted the juice in them. There was no pure water, the Japs had overrun the tank we used to swim in and cut off the supply. Of course there was plenty of water about, but it was rough and we didn't want to drink it unless we were forced to. We also took some army biscuits; they were rock hard but we took them anyway and that was it. At least we had something to eat, we had to make sure of that; we were not certain when or if, we would get any more food. We staggered and stumbled along the tracks that were used by the Nagas, swearing all the way; that seemed to help. Of course, it was pouring down with rain as usual and we were in total darkness. All we could see was the silhouette of the hills against a very dark sky, but we could hear the sound of gunfire and see flashes from the weapons in the distance. Normally, we would have mustered up a certain amount of humour to break the monotony of the situation, but for some reason we weren't up to it on that occasion. We travelled all through that night and all next day. Progress was very slow. We had to be careful, the Japs were everywhere and were infiltrating into the hills to overlook Imphal that was in the valley below. They had already taken control of the hills on the other side of the area, so it was touch and go as to whether we would get through. At that stage we were reluctant to think of the next minute and lived life by the second. It made us very alert.

We reached the perimeter of the defended 'box' in the late evening. It was dark and we were making our way through some bamboo thickets when a Gurkha suddenly appeared out of nowhere and stuck a rifle in my chest. He demanded the password for the day, but we didn't know it. We had a hell of a time trying to convince the Gurkhas we were British. We didn't look British with our long hair, beards and generally scruffy appearance. We were covered in mud as well. We had to wait until they found a British Gurkha officer. When he came, he wanted to know why we didn't know the password. By now we'd had enough, so I told him why in a few short words and that seemed to do the trick. We filtered into the 'box', found a patch of clear ground lay down and went to sleep straight away; we were absolutely exhausted. We took our boots off to give our feet an airing and it was pelting down with rain, but by then we didn't care. The next morning we tipped the water out and put our boots back on. This went on for a week until we pinched some tents that had been lying about. The Gurkha officer sent half a bucket of tea over to us when we woke up the next morning. It was the first we'd had for over four days. It was liquid gold. I think of it even now with pleasure.

We decided to try and make some contact with our unit, so we scouted around to where the most activity was and found our CO; he'd been looking for us. He knew our other mates were still down at the airstrip, but had heard nothing about the Indian officers and the sepoys, so asked us to search for them and meet back up with him in four hours. By then he hoped he could get something organised. The army had set up a field kitchen in the centre of the box and the first thing we did was to go there. We were starving and managed to get some mugs of tea and hot corned beef fritters; they tasted real good. It was the first hot food we had eaten for a long time. We rounded up some of the officers and sepoys and made our rendezvous with the CO. He took us to a flat area somewhere nearby and said that was the new hospital site. We had two days to be operational. You could have cut the silence with a knife. We were dumbfounded. However, a miracle took place and within two days and nights a tented hospital was erected ready to admit patients. It seems almost unbelievable now, but it's true. Beds were available for a thousand patients at first, but at our peak, when things were really bad, we had over two thousand in the tents. Stretchers were put on the floor in between the beds, anywhere really, where the men could be treated. They were impossible working conditions. We unclipped and left the sides of the tents up during the hot, dry days in an attempt to keep the patients as cool as possible. The Indian lads were very good, well trained and efficient. Latrines were dug, cookhouses built, in fact they did everything that was needed regarding the labour side of things. It really was hard labour. Tons of material had to be gathered together. It was scattered all over the area. Huge marquees were put up and it was raining all the time as usual. No one slept much. We hadn't got any quarters. We'd had to give up the tents we nicked to the Command Headquarters. We slept on the ground when we could, but that was out of sheer exhaustion most of the time. The rest of the lads who had been on the airstrip running the casualty post joined us. They had been merged with some medics that had been flown in from the Arakan in south-west Burma, where it was not quite so hectic at the time. Our twenty British lads completely organised the fitting out of the wards, obtaining instruments, bandages and anything they could get their hands on. Blankets weren't a problem, but we didn't have any sheets and for a while no mattresses either. The poor patients had to lie on straw filled palliasses.

We used a medium sized tent for the operating theatre such as it was. It was very basic, all we had were three antique operating tables, paraffin lamps and one small Tilley lamp. We used Primus stoves for sterilising the instruments. For sterilising gowns and gloves (when we had them) we used a small autoclave, converted from a flame-thrower. The engineers sorted that out for us. To get us up and running we had an airdrop of medical supplies. Whoever organised it did a good job. We got just what we wanted. "Let's hope it continues", somebody said. Unfortunately it didn't. In fact it became very hit and miss indeed. There was no posh opening ceremony for the hospital, the patients just came and didn't stop coming either. In less than two days we had nearly a thousand casualties. First of all it was panic, then chaos. There was no time to stand there wringing hands in despair. We didn't have time for that, we just got stuck in. People were dying. After a while, we could see a glimmer of light as things started to get into some sort of order.

We were short of drinking water when we reached the defended box after climbing over the mountains. We dug a hole in the ground for the water to collect, but it was far from clear, so we used a bush hat to filter the mud out. Bill Aspery thought it was a great idea until he realised it was his hat we were using. Then he called us for everything. Another time the latrines were full so they were filled in. Nobody bothered about it much. A layer of soil was thrown over the top to stop the flies. Somebody put Reg Hiley's hat on a stump sticking out of the morass. He saw it later on and went to fetch it. He was a little on the plump side and sank into the soil and the contents underneath; he went in to about four feet. He was only five foot six so there wasn't a lot of him sticking out, but what there was certainly made a lot of noise. I could have told him what would happen, but he didn't ask and it didn't seem right to interfere. When he emerged he was in a right mess and he wasn't amused. Everybody stared until the smell hit them, then we all started to snigger, but not for long. He pulled out his revolver and started firing at us. I'm glad to say he was in so much of a rage that his hand was unsteady and he didn't hit anyone. In any case we had taken to the jungle. We didn't fancy hanging around and we left him to cool off.

Once it was known that the Japs were concentrating all their troops to take Kohima and Imphal, we had some troops sent up from the Arakan front by air. They left the plane and went straight into battle; it must have been terrible. After the war I found that a near neighbour was one of these troops and he said it was the worst situation he had ever been in; the losses in his outfit were shocking, with more than forty percent of them being killed in a very short period. Our troops in the area had consolidated and had set up the defensive 'box' as best they could. It was to become a last stand. If the Japs broke through in any force, then that was it; it would be every man for himself. We were told to send home any note money we had and to destroy any letters or anything that might be of use to the Japanese. With these cheering thoughts ringing through my head, I sent twenty pounds home by telegraph. It never got there. Anyway, I claimed it after the war. It appeared that it had reached Bombay and was still there waiting to be claimed. Apparently, they had lost the forwarding address. The army postal service took the matter up and eventually recovered it for me. It came at the right time too, I wasn't rolling in money. Twenty pounds was a considerable amount of money then.

The hospital was situated in the middle of the box to give maximum protection. It was also near the airstrip, which was not necessarily a good thing because we were getting daily air raids and the airstrip was a prime target. The drill at the hospital was put into order of priority and as soon as the casualties arrived they were sorted out. We dealt with the surgical cases. Two of my mates would put them on plasma drips and look after them before bringing them into the operating theatre. It was like a production line in the theatre. All three tables were being used at the same time; one case being prepared, one being operated on and one being sewn up and bandaged. Afterwards, if the patient was up to it, he would be flown out to a safer area. We found out later that a lot of patients died en route because of lack of attention and the distances involved.

We managed to acquire some more tents. They were bivouac types, just big enough for two men. There was not much room, but at least we were out of the perpetual rain and it was a break from being permanently wet from sleeping outside all the time. We improvised as we went along and managed to get our own supply of tea going together with several other improvements. The field unit plus the Indian cookhouse served the patients. We couldn't do it; we had enough on our hands just treating them. One of our problems was getting a change of clothes. All our kit was at the site we had quickly evacuated and we only had what we stood up in and that was falling to bits. It was past being washed ages ago and our boots were a waste of time, the soles were held on with string. We had a meeting with the CO and he said the defensive line near the old hospital was still holding so we could try to get our kitbags plus those belonging to the officers and would we also bring back as much equipment as possible. The next morning away we went, ten of us, some sepoys and six trucks. We went along temporary roads that the Engineers had made to supply the troops in the trenches up at the front. We by-passed the Japanese road block and managed to get in through the back way to the old hospital site. It was a risky business because the Japs could see us and started firing mortars to try to stop us. Fortunately they fell short. We worked very quickly and managed to get a fair amount of stuff out, including some of our kit. However, a lot of it had gone. Some of the forward troops had been having a lucky dip. You couldn't blame them. We wondered why the Japs hadn't destroyed the hospital, then it dawned on us that they wanted it for themselves, but when they saw us ransacking it, they started firing. We decided to move out fast, the shells were getting too close and we couldn't risk staying any longer. An infantry officer told us the front line was to be moved back to secure our position and the hospital would then be in Jap hands. I suggested that we set fire to it. He agreed and we did. It didn't half go up. The hospital was made of bamboo and thatch it burnt a treat and we made sure the Japs couldn't salvage anything.

On 15th April we had a bad air attack. The Japs came over in force and dropped bombs at random. It was such a small area they couldn't miss. Their main target was the airstrip, but because we were so close, we got some of the mis-aimed bombs and were targeted ourselves. Two planes strafed with machine guns and dropped bombs on the hospital. That did a lot of damage and killed some of the patients. It didn't surprise us. It was typical of the Japs. They took no notice even though we had a Red Cross flag spread on the ground. We took it up in the end; it just seemed to make it easier for the Japs to use as a landmark. I was in my tent at the time of the raid. I had just finished three days and nights non-stop in the operating theatre. I also had a dose of malaria. I was really exhausted and looking back, I think they were the worst days of my life. I could usually get by, but this time there was nothing left. Suddenly, a row of bullets went down the tent each side of me and because of the way I was feeling, I couldn't have cared less. I didn't have the strength to run anywhere and so I just lay there, under a pile of blankets with a high temperature, shaking with cold, even though it was ninety degrees outside. My mates came in later, to see if I was all right and when they saw what had happened they laughed their heads off. Actually, they were very concerned, but I suppose it was their way of coping with the situation. They had been trying to clear up the mess that had been caused by the air raid and I can assure you that was not a nice job. You have to be real hard when you see the state of some of the casualties. It's times like that when you realise the true meaning of life and death. The only anti aircraft gun we had fired so many shells during the raid that the barrel bent and put it out of action. If it wasn't the Japs it was something else. Two nights later a cyclone hit us and half the hospital was blown down. There was a real panic and all the fit troops were hanging on to the ropes of the marquees trying to save them. Fortunately, there were no serious injuries, but my own tent was found a quarter of a mile away in some trees. My mate was asleep in it. It gave him a real fright and he wondered what the hell had happened; he thought a bomb had fallen on it. I was in the operating theatre at the time; we were trying to operate, hoping the tent wouldn't take off.

I developed a jungle sore on my left ankle and it wouldn't heal. I had it for six weeks, caused either by a bamboo splinter or a leech I had knocked off accidentally and it had left its teeth in me. All the lads had some sort of ailment or irritation, it was part of what went on out there, malaria, dysentery, sores and numerous skin complaints. You had to put them out of your mind and get on with things, but we kept moaning about them to each other. That seemed to help. I seemed to be getting over my bout of malaria. It wasn't a pleasant experience. It was such a disabling disease and put an awful lot of troops out of action. You started feeling cold and really shivered and had a tremendous temperature, with a craving to drink lots of water, pints and pints of it. Then you got the shakes and even though the temperature of your body was over a hundred and four degrees, you felt ice cold; you just couldn't get warm at all. After a while, hopefully, the fever broke and the sweating started. The sweat just flowed out, it even poured out of the ends of your fingers and saturated everything around you. Even your clothes had to be wrung out and there was always a putrid smell like burnt flesh. This went on for at least three times at twelve hourly intervals and if you didn't sweat and the fever didn't break, the temperature got higher and higher. Then, it became certain death unless you could get some ice or have a cold bath to lower the temperature, plus expert attention, which was difficult when you were in a trench.

It's difficult to imagine the conditions where we were. The terrain is so hard to describe. It was as though huge waves of an angry ocean had suddenly turned to rock and then covered themselves with primeval jungle, which stretched for miles and miles, almost impenetrable. It was a land that had never been explored. The bamboo was about a foot thick, vast areas of it and the valleys were just huge swamps. Then there's the wildlife; the snakes being the worst and insects that have never been catalogued. They all seemed vicious to us because we had never seen anything of the kind before. I suppose, thinking about it now, it was a naturalist's paradise; if he could survive in it. It held a strange fascination that I shall never forget. Most troops who were out there felt the same. It was like looking back in time, as things used to be.

The railway finished at Dimapur, and it was by road after that and there was only one decent one from India into North Burma and that went to Imphal. The distance was one hundred and thirty four miles of single-track road, hewn out of the sides of mountains and very unreliable, especially during the monsoon. From Imphal it was twenty-eight miles of rough track road to Palel and from there to Tamu was fifty six miles of mule pack track and that's as far as we went at that time. The Japs held the rest of Burma. That road was the only decent ground supply route and was in continuous use. The lorries were only five tonners, which was just as well. The road couldn't take anything heavier. The lorries would run around the clock bringing supplies to the troops, then bringing back any wounded. Any lorry that broke down and couldn't be repaired quickly would be stripped of its contents and pushed over the side into the jungle below. The road had to be kept open at all times. It was critical to get the supplies through. On occasion the road slipped and supplies had to be carried by men across the gap. This was a frequent occurrence. All troops in the area were put on half rations. A temporary repair was made but it soon collapsed again and this went on until the monsoons stopped and the mountain dried out. It was the same in other areas too, the road was never reliable, the tonnage required of it was too much. A lot of the mountain was made up of loose shale and very difficult to stabilise and since this was the only road into Burma, you can imagine the problems the Engineers and transport sections had. Some goods were flown in and that helped, but the amount was very small and they were generally only urgent supplies.

It was 20th April 1944 and the battles around us were going non-stop. The Japs needed Imphal and Kohima to get into India, and were going flat out to take them. The 14th army was doing its best to halt their advance, but the conditions were shocking. The artillery had positioned about a hundred, twenty-five 'pounder' guns in a clearing just a few yards away from our tents and they banged away night and day. The noise was incredible and that, together with our non-stop work, meant a complete lack of sleep. I remember saying to my mate, that if ever I got out of this mess, I would sleep for a week. It was a particularly difficult time. There weren't many smiling faces; everything was taken very seriously. The Japs sent air raids twice a day and we were on quarter rations. Things were getting really bad. We had no fresh food at all, not even for the patients, just corned beef or corned mutton and army type, hard biscuits. The heat affected the tins of meat and when we opened them, the contents had liquefied and came out all runny. It looked revolting and tasted the same, the cook did his best, but we always ended up having rissoles, nothing else except, of course, hot sweet tea. There was no respite in the fighting over the next few days. It was as fierce as ever, with no quarter given by either side. We were outnumbered and short of supplies and the conditions, for both armies, were atrocious. It continued to rain both day and night and the mud was thick puddingy stuff. You got worn out walking in it. It got everywhere and it smelt too, a rancid damp smell; Canal No.5 we called it. At Kohima, not far away, the same was going on. It was a question of which fell first, Imphal or Kohima; or perhaps a miracle would happen, we would survive? We were still getting air raids, but had recently got hold of a few Hurricane fighter planes. There was some real dog fights between them and the Jap Zeros. Our pilots usually won and it was great to watch.

According to the Japanese, Imphal was on the verge of collapse. It was 26th April and they reckoned it would be captured by the Emperor's birthday on 29th April. They threw everything they had at us; attack after attack. They were going berserk in an effort to break through. All our troops were on full alert and everyone was armed, including any patients who could hold a gun and use it. All the staff were armed too. In the operating theatre I had a Sten gun plus a revolver and spare ammunition. My mate had the same. The officers had an assortment of weapons plus some grenades. We certainly would have used them too because if the Japs got in, they would have shot anyone on sight. So, it was a question of shoot or be shot. Of course, that left us on edge, especially at night. We lived on our nerves. We were ready to shoot at the slightest noise.

Well, the big day for the Japs came, April 29th, the Emperor's birthday and we were all waiting in trepidation wondering what they would do. We knew they would give it everything and they did. They attacked all round the defended 'box'. The whole area was only ten miles across and the conditions were terrible. They were fanatical, screaming and shouting as they attacked. The noise of gunfire was terrific and it kept going all day and night. The Jap planes came continuously and dropped bombs anywhere. Our Hurricanes were having a go at them, trying to fend them off, so the Japs just dropped their load and flew off. Despite the enemy's superior numbers, both in weapons and men, the 'box' held. We had few dents here and there, but by and large it was contained, albeit with a very high cost in casualties. There was no retreat. We didn't give any ground. Mind you there was nowhere to go. It was all very final; a last stand. I remember at the time that no one said much about the possibility of being overrun by the Japs, but I know it was on everybody's mind and I honestly think that is why our troops gave such a super human effort. There was no shirking, they gave everything they had; plus that little bit extra that made all the difference.

The three tables in the theatre tent were tended by Lt. Colonel Surgeon Langhorne, a Major Surgeon, an anaesthetist, two trainee Indian doctors, two Indian orderlies, two operating assistants, my mate, Bill Aspery and me and of course, the corporal in charge. Outside there was a reception tent, next to the theatre and two of my pals worked there. It was their job to sort out the casualties as they came in and put them in some sort of priority. That was a job in itself as all the cases were urgent and virtually all of them were on plasma drips. Blood was out of the question, we had no way of keeping it. There were no fridges, no electric lights either, only oil lamps; all very basic. Still, the casualties kept coming and with the fighting so close by. The injured were brought in on stretchers, straight from where they had fallen. All they had been given was a quarter gram of morphine and the lads who worked with the forward troops marked this on their forchead in indelible ink. These particular medics were very brave chaps and worked in extreme danger when you consider the Japs shot at anything that moved. When they reached us, the patients were put to sleep, boots and socks removed and all their clothes cut off and an estimate the damage undertaken. We would then start on repairing the damage, starting with the worst things first, as most casualties had more than one injury. It was a good job we didn't have time to think too much, it would have sent us crackers. We soon learned to be tolerant and patient realising that you lived minute by minute and understood how frail life really was. I assisted at all the operations and the surgeon, Lieutenant Colonel Langhorne and myself formed an inseparable team. I knew exactly what he wanted during the operations, which instruments, sutures, everything and, as important, his method of working. It was fantastic to see him make decisions bearing in mind he knew nothing about the case until it came on to the table. The injuries were horrific; arms and legs had to be amputated, terrible head wounds, some blinded and lots of severe body injuries. It was very sad and tragic to see bodies mutilated so much. Some had flash burns and these were awful, with sections of the body just melted away. As soon as we finished one case we would move to the next table and so on. This just went on and on until we either ran out of medical supplies or collapsed from sheer exhaustion, whichever came first. I remember at one stage that we went three days and nights without stopping; we looked like ghosts and felt awful. I don't know what kept us going. We did all we could with as much dedication as possible, but sadly, in a lot of cases, this wasn't enough. The inevitable happened and lives were lost. We developed a cold and clinical exterior, but inwardly it was very heart searching.

The conditions in the operating tent were really primitive, we had tarpaulin cover on the floor, and this was always covered in a sea of mud. It never stopped raining enough for it to get dry. All the sterilising was done with the aid of Primus stoves, and these were very hit and miss. The instruments we had were never out of the steriliser, the knives and needles were kept in a solution of Lysol; the plaster of Paris came loose in drums, so we used to get the patients, where possible, to put it on the bandages for us. Everything was home made. Even the dirty bandages were washed, boiled and used again. This is where the Indian orderlies came in; they were very good, and would be standing by waiting for the used instruments, wash them and put them back in the steriliser. They also supplied us with endless cups of tea. At first we wore white hats and gowns and masks, but these got cut up and used for bandages, so we had rubber aprons. These were more practical and could be washed and used all the time. We only ever wore a pair of shorts and boots underneath. The lighting in the theatre was really something else, paraffin lamps with wicks and a large Tilley lamp with a mantle. It was great while it worked, but it had a nasty habit of blowing up in the middle of an operation and blazing paraffin would start cascading down on to us. I could move quite fast in those days. It was just as well. In spite of these very poor conditions our success rate was very good. We did really save a lot of lives although we were desperately short of supplies. We used to crush sulphanilamide tablets into powder and put it in and on the wounds and we rarely had stitch abscesses. I used to do quite a lot of the stitching up myself as the surgeon was sizing up the next case and during that time he would leave me to finish off. I got quite good at it in the end. After treatment, the worst cases would stay with us for a few days, but where possible, we flew the others out as soon as we could; we needed the beds and the bandages for new cases. Despite that, at any one time, we had over twelve hundred patients in our charge.

It was May 1st and there was no change at the front. The Japs were still trying to get into Imphal. Their mortar shells and canon fire came very close. We knew the whole area needed help very soon and the only supplies were by air, either to the airstrip or by parachute. Rations became very tight and the water tasted horrible. Each day was the same, nothing seemed to change. Then, a few days later we had a supply drop which included a small amount of mail, sent as morale booster by the higher ups. We hadn't received mail for a long time and were looking forward to it. Mind you, it didn't do some of the lads any good. They received 'Dear John' letters, a term used by troops when their girlfriends or wives had found someone else. In fact, there were only twenty soldiers in our contingent and eighteen of them, including myself, had one of these letters. It didn't upset the single lads so much but the married ones were devastated. I felt the problem lay in the fact that the letters sent home were so heavily censored that it made the contents a bit flat. We couldn't say where we were, not even comment on the weather, not even which country we were in, nothing of interest really. All the reader knew was that we were with SEAC, which meant South East Asia Command; well that was no good. This and the fact that many of the letters never reached home tended to make people feel forgotten on both sides and there was no home leave for anyone; what could you expect? In fact, in the four years I was in the Far East, all I had was fourteen days survivor's leave in Calcutta after Imphal was relieved. I wasn't even allowed home.

We had been under siege for a month and still the situation remained the same. We felt something would have to crack soon. You could feel the intensity of the pressure daily and we were desperately trying to make certain it wouldn't be us giving in first. The Japs took a hill overlooking the airstrip and managed to consolidate the position. This was very serious because if they put the airstrip out of action it would have been all over for us. It was our only means of supply. Fortunately, we had got hold of a Vengeance dive-bomber that had recently arrived in India. It was just the job and came loaded with huge bombs. It circled and then dived and dropped the lot, smack on top of the hill. At the same time about ninety, twenty five-pound guns went into action. It was incredible, the top of the hill was blown right off. It was a fantastic sight, really morale boosting. The Japs were scattering in all directions, in absolute chaos. Then some of our lads moved in, plus some Ghurkas and after a very fierce battle managed to kill all the Japs. They had a hell of a job though. The Japs fought till the death, never gave up; "it was a great honour to die for the Emperor!" We could see the action from the hospital and prepared for the casualties and there were plenty of those. When the action was over, everybody stood and cheered. You could feel the relief because we all realised that it could have been so different and that didn't bear thinking about. However, what it did do was to give a big boost to our morale and believe me we needed it. Perhaps this was the turning point; we hoped so.

It was May 14th and we were still besieged. The wounded still came in and kept coming. We were working twenty hours a day, every day, snatching sleep when we could. I hadn't slept in my tent for over a week, I just lay down on some blankets in the theatre. The monsoons arrived the next day which meant the weather would get worse than it normally was and that wasn't good. The thunderstorms were terrific and the rain came down so hard that our normal mud was now super mud with a super smell. Everything went crazy; small streams became raging torrents and took away everything in their path. It was spectacular to see, but we could have done without it. Nothing much altered over the next few days. The food was still scarce, just bully beef and hard biscuits, but still fortunately lots of hot sweet tea. The rains were getting worse and Jap and British troops were at a standstill, nothing could move in that sea of mud and virtually all aircraft were grounded, which meant no supplies. It was much the same throughout the rest of the month, violent thunderstorms and continuous rain, non-stop days and nights. We hadn't had dry clothes for weeks. We were soaking wet all the time. We used to tip our boots upside down when we went to sleep otherwise they got full of water; not that it mattered that much, sleep was a luxury and we didn't have a lot. Sleeping in two man bivouac tents that were so old and battered was like sleeping in a colander. Yet we considered ourselves lucky when you think that the infantry were standing in their trenches all the time in that diabolical weather, with no chance of being relieved. It must have been really awful. There were no spare men. Everyone was on permanent stand to.

We heard that the Japs were infiltrating into the Bishenpur area south of Imphal. That was May 28th. No Bank Holiday break for us. It was quite easy for them in that type of country with the dense undergrowth, thick bamboo and very tall grasses; just right for ambushes and I must say the Japs were good at that. It appeared that this would be the big one, the Japs had tried all round the Imphal Box to get in but had been held off by our troops. Now, the Japs had been told to take it regardless of cost. A fantastic battle took place with all available troops taking part. Although our morale was high, our troops began to fade and would need help soon. This wasn't any regular battle. It sapped the men's physical endurance, taking place in some of the worst terrain in the world and against a very formidable, tenacious enemy. These Japs were fanatical; they didn't know when or how to give in. They would rather die than surrender and many did just that. Even with terrible injuries they would still try and fight on. They just had to be killed and our chaps obliged. It was either them or us. This went on for some days, but in the end both the Japs and ourselves had to withdraw because the area was so bad with the stench of rotting bodies. The vultures and rats had a field day. It was war at its worst.

At the beginning of June more troops were flown in from the Arakan. As they get off the planes they went straight into action. That's how near they were to the front line. They walked straight into a sea of mud and total darkness. There was no transport, that was all bogged down. Nothing could move. You would walk ten yards and it seemed like a mile. It was exhausting. The bigger guns had to be dismantled and carried up the hills piece by piece and the shells too of course. It must have been a tremendous shock for them. Four or five days later we were still cut off but more planes were coming in, including some big American supply planes loaned from the China front; also some more Hurricanes, Spitfires and Mitchell bombers. These were really good to see. It raised our morale no end. The Jap air raids got less and less as our planes continued knocking the hell out of them. I chatted to some troops that had been relieved for a short spell and they said the Japs were starting to crack. They had lost thousands of men. We were told that the 14th army wouldn't fight during the monsoons, but we did, so we took what we heard with a pinch of salt but at least there was now hope. General Slim said there was to be no let up, we must keep going. We all thought he was raving mad but he was right. If we hadn't we would have certainly been overrun and either killed or captured.

Two Casualty Clearing Stations had been flown in from India and were set up by the airstrip. This relieved the pressure on us and we put them in charge of air evacuation. These new medics were raw to battle conditions and couldn't believe what they saw and were horrified at the working conditions. They learned quickly out there. It was the 19th June and we were still cut off, still on half rations, still working twenty hours a day. The theatre was like a butcher's shop and every case needed major surgery; arms off, legs off, sometimes both; bayonet wounds, bullet wounds, horrendous burns and lots of head injuries. It went on and on, every day and every night. We never knew what to expect. They brought the bodies onto the operating table. We put the chaps to sleep and then we started. Many a time we got half way through a repair job and found that the patient had died. That is when you had to be very hard and just move to the next table and start all over again. You couldn't afford to think. Sometimes I saw my mate in the reception area and would ask if there were any more cases. He looked at me and just said, "Yes!" That one little word could fill volumes; we both knew its true meaning. The wounded kept coming. We were all feeling the strain of this non-stop onslaught and even our instruments were beginning to wear out. We were rapidly running out of equipment and because of the weather it wasn't always possible to get an air drop, so we had to improvise. It was quite incredible what we did, adapting and repairing things to keep going.

Great news arrived on 23rd June, the road between Kohima and Imphal had been reopened. The 2nd Dagger Division and the 5th Division of the 14th army had met up with each other and all the Japs had been cleared from the road area. They were still about though, but were slowly retreating. Everybody cheered like mad, some cried with joy and relief. Things were still bad, but at least we were now able to get some supplies through from India to keep going. Since 31st March to 23rd June, we had been in a state of siege with no way in and no way out, except by air and this was very hit and miss because of the weather and the lack of aircraft. It was pure survival. We spent eighty-five days there in all and that's a long time with every day being uncertain as to what the outcome would be. Having said that, we weren't sure whether we would make it. The Japs were far from beaten and still too close for comfort.

CHAPTER SIX

All our supplies had to be flown in during the siege. As the planes were unloaded they were refilled with wounded troops to be flown out to other hospitals. It was the only way to move the injured. The Japs were everywhere. One hundred and eighty thousand cases were evacuated by this method. Not all the men had suffered with wounds, some were non combatants so were airlifted to save supplies. Many had caught one or more of the tropical diseases that were rife. The health of the troops was causing great anxiety with incidences of malaria and dysentery as high as seventy five percent at times and having a dramatic effect on the troops available for action. In the end they put most camps on high ground and stopped using the valleys in an effort to escape the mosquitoes, but they thrived in the wet hot humid conditions and were ever present. The casualties from malaria were still very high. Dysentery was another killer, it was terrible; shocking stomach pains, non stop diarrhoea; you became very dehydrated and lost a great deal of weight and nearly all your energy. The army sanitary squads did fantastic work regarding sanitation and mosquito control, but it was always a losing battle. There were millions of other flies and these caused a constant spread of dysentery, which was virtually uncontrollable. You had to take precautions all the time; the water needed boiling or sterilising with special tablets and all uncooked food had to be washed in potassium permanganate crystals. Another thing we had to be careful about was tetanus and although all the troops were inoculated against it, we still had a few cases appear from time to time, probably because they missed their booster injections. They had to be cared for by the medical side of the hospital. We had to keep it out of the theatre. We couldn't take any chances. They were supposed to be kept quiet. The slightest noise would send them rigid from head to toe. With the noise of a battle going on nearby they didn't respond too well and unfortunately most of them died.

The CO had us all on parade the day after the road was reopened and shook hands with us all, thanking us for what we had done and said we would have a rest as soon as reinforcements arrived. In the meantime however, we were to carry on. The opening of the road was just the start. It meant we could get some of the supplies that had been building up at Dimapur. The first to arrive was ammunition; guns and military hardware including some light tanks, plus medical equipment for which we were desperate and of course, more troops, mostly veterans that had fought all the way up from Dimapur. The next day the cook went to collect our rations and came back with a live sheep. It was the first fresh meat for over three months, but it was a real mangy scraggy thing. It looked as though it had walked all the way from India and only just had the strength to stand up. You wouldn't believe it, but of all the tough guys there and after what we had been through, nobody had the bottle to kill it. We could have shot it all right but it needed to be bled and the usual way was to stun it and then cut its throat. Not one of us could bring ourselves to do it, so we asked a Gurkha to kill it for us. That wasn't a pretty sight, all he did was to get out his kukri (knife) and chop its head off with one blow, not quite what we wanted or expected, but the job was done. Then it had to be dressed and cleaned out by someone and most of the lads vanished. I was assigned the task because of my job in the operating theatre; apparently I was suited to it? Anyway, I con-scripted one of my mates to help and we hung the carcass by its back legs on a branch of a tree and dug a hole underneath. Everything we didn't want went into that. There didn't seem a lot left, but what there was, I chopped up into pieces and gave it to the cook. He prodded it and jokingly asked how was it cooked as he had only ever cooked corned beef. He did his best with it and served it up with great ceremony. It was really tough, even the gravy wasn't up to much, but it was meat and we intended to enjoy it. He made a stew with the left overs but it didn't get any tenderer. After what we had eaten over the past few months it was a welcome change. Things did improve a little and one of the best was the setting up of some mobile ovens for making bread. We didn't get a lot, but what we had was marvellous, the first for over four months. We didn't have butter or margarine though, just a type of semi liquid vegetable fat called 'gee'. It was really horrible stuff, but it was all there was. When I look back' I wonder what we did eat half the time. It certainly wasn't a lot nor very often and never particularly tasty but I think we were more interested in survival than the quality of the next meal.

Despite our change in fortune, the Japs were still around in force, but our troops seemed to be holding them, in fact, they were steadily push-ing them back, very slowly though because of the appalling conditions and lack of supplies. Although the road was open, we still depended on air supplies, but they were delayed because of the low clouds and atro-cious weather. There was no let up in the amount of casualties either, but at least we all seemed happier and morale was a little higher. It seemed that things were getting that little bit better, thank God.

Some of the fresh troops that had been flown in from India just looked at us in amazement. We weren't surprised, we must have looked as though we had emerged from a graveyard; thin, dirty, knackered, long hair and beards, our clothes in tatters and having acquired that strange yellow colour due to the mepacrine tablets to ward off malaria. It didn't take them long to see why we were in such a state, the Japs were only ten miles away and were gathering for another attack, so they were soon to get a taste of what a regular day at Imphal was like. With troops and more armour coming in daily, the Japs were going to find things tough and although the Japanese radio said they would take Imphal within a week, we were now more confident that they wouldn't. Things contin-ued to improve, but the casualties kept coming, mainly from the Ukhrul area. It was terrible to see the waste of life and the horrendous injuries sustained by the men, some of which would affect them for the rest of their lives. A lot more of the patients were flown to Comilla. The 14th British General Hospital was now set up there after their hurried evacua-tion from Imphal and was now in full operation. That pleased us because it only took a couple of hours by air; by road it took weeks in very haz-ardous conditions. It was a terrible feeling to learn that someone had died on the road back to India because of lack of medical attention, after we had worked so hard to keep them alive. We sent all our medical cases back, that was those men that suffered from illness rather than battle injury or were recovering from a wound; it gave us more room for surgi-cal cases. As our troops pushed the Japs back the wounded were coming in the worse for wear, due to that little extra distance to reach us and lack of attention at the front. Four of our chaps volunteered to go and form a Field First Aid Post, so that we could get the cases back in slightly better condition. They usually put them on plasma drips and gave them a shot of morphine. It really helped.

July 15th was quite a day. I was called to the CO's office. The Colonel there said I had been promoted to Corporal, two stripes and back dated ninety days which was worth a few quid. It was war substantiated too, so they couldn't take my stripes away. If that wasn't enough I had been granted fourteen days 'survivors' leave as had my mate, Bill Aspery, who worked in the theatre with me. In fact those that worked in the theatre, including the officers and surgeons were given it. Our places at the hospital were being taken over by some medics, four operating assistants, flown in from the Middle East. In the meantime, a lot of cases were being sent to 53rd IGH, which had been sent in to help out.

We decided to take our leave in Calcutta and on our way, Bill and I were told we would go by air to Comilla in two separate planes. I was to be put in charge of some special cases, which turned out to be injured Jap officers and Bill, was put in charge of a number of serious head injuries. The planes we went in were DC3s, cargo type, but had been fitted out as air ambulances. The stretchers were strapped all round the interior. It was a bit primitive but worked. The flight over the mountains was very bumpy and with no seats we found it difficult to stand, so I sat on the floor. The sergeant who was flying the plane said that if the patients were okay I could go in the cabin and sit in the co-pilots seat, which I did. I had a fantastic view of the jungle, but then the pilot said there would be no hope of rescue if we came down in it and that was a bit unnerving. It wasn't just the terrain, the Japs were down there in force, but fortunately, they didn't have any anti-aircraft guns or fighter planes in the area and we landed safely at Comilla. I handed over the patients then went to see some of my old mates at the 14th BGH. It was great to meet up with them again. They all wanted to know how things were up at the front and we talked about the old days and better times. I then met up with Bill and we continued on our way to Calcutta to start our leave.

From Comilla, we went by rail to Chandpur, then by paddle steamer down the Brahmaputra River to Goalundo, where we arrived next day and then spent another day on the train to Calcutta. We booked in at movement control at Calcutta racecourse, which had been turned into a leave centre. In the army, your leave started when you arrived at your chosen destination, which in our case was Sunday July 16th. The longer it took for you to get there, the longer you were away from the action, so nobody rushed. We actually arrived at the special leave centre barracks at eight in the morning and I must say we were treated really well. There were about two hundred of us from the front and were the first intake into this new centre. They really tried to make it good for us and they did. The first thing we did was to have a good bath and a change of clothes, it was sheer luxury. The food was good and there were real beds with sheets. It was marvellous! In Calcutta it took some time for our stomachs to adjust to the extra food. We weren't used to it. In Imphal the food was very hit and miss, I can't remember eating much. Tea and lime juice kept me going, they kept me alive more or less. When the siege of Imphal ended I only weighed seven and a half stone; my normal weight was ten and a half. Nearly everyone had lost some weight out there, it couldn't be helped in the conditions.

Calcutta was an extraordinary place, situated on the banks of the Hooghly River. The city covered a massive area. It was absolutely teeming with life, you couldn't imagine how they all managed to live there. There was an enormous amount of poverty and squalor. Beggars were everywhere. Most of the railway stations were occupied by permanent groups of families who were born, lived and died there. They used to sleep on the platforms amongst the rubbish and noise. There were huge rats running about but no one cared, I don't suppose they had any choice in the matter. Although we didn't like it, we accepted it as their way of life and after what we had witnessed we were hardened to those situations.

We went sightseeing around Calcutta straight away. We went to 'Smokey Joes', a non-Indian café, a bit of a haunt for the troops on leave at the time. We ordered steak and all the trimmings and what a meal it was; a huge piece of steak, six eggs and loads of assorted vegetables and chips. I hadn't seen a meal like it since leaving Durban. It was so big that Bill and I couldn't eat it all, our stomachs just would not take it, we had been on such low rations for so long. But it was great to taste good food again. We even went to the cinema, which was quite modern by Indian standards. We went there most days because it was free for the troops on leave and they had flown in the latest films from America.

There were no summer time hours out there and it got dark quite early, so at night we would go to the naafi or a small hotel bar. There weren't any pubs as we knew them. The place to go was called the Chowringee. Everybody went there. We all noticed the increase of the prices of things since we first came. There were a lot of Americans about as well and they always seemed to have more money than we did. They were mainly top motor mechanics and had put a track down the side of the main street. The track was about a mile long, just like those in a factory. All types of army vehicles that were the worst for wear were put on one end and came off the other, like a new vehicle. It was good to watch them. They would strip a vehicle down to the chassis, then rebuild it as it moved along the track.

At the centre there was a marvellous swimming pool and I swam in it every day. It was really refreshing and one of the few ways of keeping cool. It was probably one of the few things I did everyday because we only had fourteen days and we tried to cram in as much as possible. We went to Calcutta Zoo, which was situated, on the banks of the river. It had a huge selection of animals, some I had never seen before. It was a real education. As our stomachs got used to it, our intake of food started to get better and we went to Chinese restaurants for a change. They were very good and we could get English type food there too, quite a nice experience. We also played golf, table tennis, snooker, darts, anything to make the most of things and in the evening we went to the shows put on by ENSA, the forces entertainment services. They were very good too and gave us something to laugh about. Bill and I went everywhere in Calcutta; you name it, we went there. On one occasion we went to a hotel called the Casanova, a typical meeting place for troops. There were about five hundred Yanks there and a lot of Scottish troops, veterans of Burma, plus other soldiers on leave. The dance floor was tiny and there were only six Anglo-Indian girls there barely dressed and of course, everyone tried to dance with them. It was a case of three steps then change partners. As the blokes butted in during the dances, one thing led to another and a fantastic fight broke out over these girls. It was the British versus the Yanks and just like a wild west show; tables and chairs were thrown and broken; all the windows and mirrors smashed. Anything that moved was thrown at someone or somewhere else. My mate Bill was absolutely legless with booze and I'd had a fair whack myself, but was on my feet, so I picked him up, flung him over my shoulder and ran out through a smashed window. Then the Red Caps and US Military Police arrived and immediately everyone scattered. You don't argue with them. They would throw you into a wagon and you would spend the rest of your leave in prison. Afterwards the hotel was closed down. I don't know whether it was because of the trouble or because of the cost to repair it. Nevertheless, it was a hell of a fight, the best I have ever seen, just like in the films. All troops on leave had to be back in their barracks by 23.50 pm, so we used to travel back from the town on tongas, horse drawn two wheeled carriages. It was two miles from town to the barracks, so we would line up the tongas, about fifty of them and have a race. The winning Tonga Wallah would be given five rupees, a lot of money to him. We did this every night. We must have been quite mad. It was very dangerous, but nobody cared. There used to be some terrific pile-ups.

A Tonga - the local Taxi

It was 31st July 1944 and, after a very enjoyable leave, we reluctantly, had to start on our journey back to Imphal. The day I started back, I weighed ten stone; not bad in fourteen days. Unfortunately it wasn't to last. We caught a train at one in the afternoon and arrived at Parbatipur at ten thirty in the evening and then caught another train to Pandu where we arrived the next morning. Eventually we boarded a river steamboat and went up the Brahmaputra River again and then by train to Dimapur a couple of days later. The journey by train from Calcutta soon entered the jungle with its wet, hot and sticky atmosphere which instantly reminded us of what we were going back to. Initially, you would tense up with the fear of the uncertain future, then one of us, usually me, would say or do something humorous to take our minds off it. It was like a reflex action. You daren't dwell on any fears or apprehensions. At Dimapur we went to the rest camp there, where we stayed until transport was available to take us to Kohima and on to Imphal. The so-called rest camp was actually a reinforcement centre and it was there Bill and I nearly landed up in the infantry. All troops lined up each morning regardless of who you were or what regiment you were in. Then an officer would count out the first twenty men and send them to a unit that needed making up to strength and then the next twenty or so to another unit and so on. Bill and I were told to report to the Royal West Kent regiment. We handed in our pay books to their company office for examination and when the officer saw them he blew a gasket. He sent for us immediately and told us we had first priority on any transport to Imphal. Medics were in such short supply in the forward areas that we were to get full co-operation everywhere we went. We learned later that we should have been flown back from Calcutta, but by the time the movement control got the message we were already on the train.

We arrived back at Imphal on August 7th, to a cheer from our mates, saw the CO who told us that all our officers were back off leave and we would take over the operating theatre in the morning. It took the first day for us to get it back to our method of working. It was a right mess to begin with, the other chaps just couldn't cope and to cap it all we had no supplies left. The theatre was closed for two days before we received any more and we were forced to send new casualties to the 38th BGH that had come in when the road was reopened. Bill and I thought there would be a load of mail for us when we returned, but there wasn't any; it had been nearly three months since we'd had some. I left Bill to wait for the supplies for the theatre, while two of the other lads and myself decided to climb the mountains at the back of the hospital that we knew were free from Japs. On top of the mountain lay a Naga village and we thought we might get some provisions there. We were a little worried about the reception we would get, but I knew some of them from the theatre, especially children who came in for minor injuries. They thought it wonderful to have a finger bandaged and would keep it on for weeks. In the end they started to become a nuisance, I'm sure they cut themselves on purpose just to get a dressing of some sort. The Nagas did not mix with any other tribe. They were a race on their own and very wild too. Prior to the war they were head-hunters. We left the tents at eight in the morning and climbed up the mountain using paths made by the Nagas. It took us till four in the afternoon to reach the top, a real stiff climb. When we eventually reached the entrance to the village, we saw a huge bamboo archway and on it hung an enormous amount of skulls, the teeth all grinning at us. There was no-one in sight, not a sound, nothing and, at first, we thought we had made a big mistake. Then, we were sure we had when some Nagas appeared, waving their spears. They must have weighed us up and seen there were only three of us; we were very worried. We had our hands on our revolvers, just in case things went wrong. Then, the head of the tribe came forward and held our hands in greeting. It was a hell of a relief. We learned later that we were the first foreigners ever to go there.

We had a 'pow-wow' as best we could and fortunately, one of them could speak a little Hindi, which together with a little sign language we got by. We were amazed at the amount of land that lay at the top of the mountain and the way they had cultivated it, by very primitive methods; there were no machines up there. It was like a little hidden city. They had everything they needed. They made us very welcome and we were shown around the village and invited to stay the night there. It was just as well because it was getting dark and we didn't fancy spending the night on the mountain side and it was too dangerous to try and climb down in the pitch black darkness. There was the threat of any animals that might be about. The Chief of the village, or 'Babu' as he was called, laid on a feast in our honour. We had roast pig, cooked over an open fire and sweet potatoes, washed down with their fermented rice beer; really a night to remember. We slept in a bamboo hut on a pile of straw. We wondered about the fleas at first, but thought so what and went to sleep. The Nagas set about their work early and the next morning about four o'clock, we were given some boiled eggs, some leavened, flat bread and some sort of greasy tea made with goats milk. We drank it though. When we had finished, we said our farewells and we gave the Babu a bag of salt. This was more precious than gold to them. They wouldn't take money. Money was no good to them. They worked on a barter system and salt was a valuable commodity. The entire village came out to see us go, the children in particular, they loved us. We'd given them some hard, ration chocolate and they thought it was marvellous. You should have seen their faces. The climb down was worse than the climb up, very rugged and steep and difficult to get a foothold. Of course, the Nagas did this every day and had wonderful physiques to show for it, but we weren't used to it at all, we were shattered. Eventually we reached our unit and nobody had missed us, they thought I was in the theatre and the others on the wards. A good job the Japs hadn't got us.

The supplies arrived and we started receiving patients again, non stop as usual and to make things worse, the rains restarted and the humidity was unbearable - things were back to normal. That leave seemed an age ago. During the next two months life went on with little change, every-thing was non-stop, but at least the food got a little better and there was a bit more of it. Unfortunately it was all tinned. There was nothing fresh except the local fruit, which was mainly mangoes.

Lord Mountbatten came to Imphal and stood on a box in the middle of the airstrip and gave a speech saying everyone had done well and the battle for Imphal was over. It was the first time the invincible Japs had suffered defeat since they had started the war. However, he said there was to be no let up, even though the monsoons were on, the Japs were on the run and it must be kept that way. We must complete the job. He said we were no longer the 'Forgotten Army' and things were going to alter, starting with more and better supplies. We hoped he was right.

Although the actual battle of Imphal was over, our troops were mov-ing forward to Tamu, Tiddim, Palel and Ukhrul and the Japs were still fighting like mad. Their Commanders were just throwing them into battle, trying not to lose face with the higher ranks. I remember I was on the way back from Tiddim during a Jap attack there. There were six of us in a jeep and suddenly we heard a whistle. A shell exploded and the road gave way. We found ourselves rolling down the side of the hill in the jeep, falling about one hundred and fifty feet in all. We managed to crawl out; one chap had a broken arm, but most of us had only cuts and bruises. It hurt though; I had a whacking great bruise on the left-hand side of my face and a cut above the eye. I tended to the chap's broken arm and we all crawled back up to the road and got a lift back to Imphal. If the engineers had time they would haul the jeep back up the cliff. If not, they would set fire to it.

With the troops moving forward it didn't make it any easier for us, in fact, it was worse because the distance from the hospital increased. Their condition was deteriorating due to the time it took to get them to us. Their wounds were often infected or maggot ridden. One night at the 41st IGH, we were told to get ready for a large convoy of injured. We got everything ready, evacuated a load of patients down the line to make room and waited with all instruments in the sterilisers, ready for action. They arrived at one in the morning, eight ambulances capable of holding twelve cases each. Corporal Rodgers, in charge of the reception tent and myself went to look and sort out the worst of the casualties, but we found every ambulance full of dead bodies. The CO went mad. The Yanks didn't know what hit them. Three of us and an officer went forward to see if better transportation of the injured could be set up. We arranged for a forward Casualty Clearing Station to be manned by British medics and for the American field service unit to use their ambulances solely for the use of injured troops. They were filling the ambulances with dead bodies just to get them away from the front in quick time, but that didn't help the injured.

Most of the wounded we received were in shocking condition and most cases were serious, but some were incredible. One such was a Gurkha that came in on a stretcher in a terrible state and at the side of him was a bundle wrapped in a blanket. We thought it was his personal belongings at first, that is until we went to move it; then we found it was his intestines. He had been bayoneted and all his intestines had fallen out. He himself, had put them into a blanket and someone found him and put him onto a stretcher and he eventually reached our hospital. We put him on the operating table and decided to put his intestines into a bucket of saline solution and wash them; there was not much seriously wrong with them, a few cuts here and there which we mended. We then checked inside his abdomen to see if all was well and then put all his intestines back into the cavity and stitched him up. We put some crushed sulphanilamide tablets inside him and also on the stitches and hoped for the best. We kept him at the hospital. The Surgeon, myself and a few others wanted to see what would happen and lo and behold, in less than four weeks he was up and about and at his own request rejoined his unit - passed his medical Grade I, so it was all worth while. I don't know what happened to him or whether he survived the war, but if he did, he had a hell of a tale to tell.

Sadly, all cases didn't have quite such a happy ending. I remember one chap who had been shot through one eye, the bullet went through the bridge of his nose and knocked out the other eye. When he came into us he was unconscious and with his other wounds was very near death, but we did what we could and he recovered. The first thing he asked was would he be blind? I had the lousy task of telling him "Yes". He said why didn't we let him die, he would have been better off?

A lot of limbs were amputated as well and it fell on me as usual to tell the men why. Some of the troops accepted what had happened, happy to be alive, others were devastated. I didn't enjoy that part of the job one bit. We had several cases of gangrene, mostly in the legs and in nearly every case it meant amputation, but in one case the gangrene had gone too far into the thigh and we couldn't do anything with it. We had slashed the leg to try and drain it but it was no good, we could only make him as comfortable as possible and wait for the inevitable. We put him into a tent on his own because of the smell. It was so bad you could smell it all over the hospital. Eventually he died. He didn't feel much pain though, he was full of morphine.

We also had trouble with an Indian NCO, he had been shell shocked and had suffered several minor wounds, but the shock had caused him to have water retention; he couldn't pass urine and it was causing him a great deal of anxiety. We tried a catheter but had no success, so the surgeon said we would have him in the theatre the next day, put him to sleep and relax him. But that night I was called to the ward by one of my mates; the poor patient was going berserk, throwing himself all over the place and screaming in agony. I went to try and pacify him and he came at me with a dagger. I could see he meant business, his predicament was driving him mad, so I thumped him straight on the jaw and he went out like a light. Then, to our amazement he started passing urine. He woke up after a few seconds and when he saw what was happening he went mad with joy and, with a great big smile, all over his face he rushed over to me, put his arms round me and thanked me. That was great for him, but not for me, he was still urinating and I was covered and so were several round about. He must have 'peed' for several minutes; it seemed an age anyway. It must have been a great relief for him as you can imagine. Afterwards, he couldn't do enough for us; he did anything we asked.

We didn't only treat the ground troops, we had a pilot in one day; his Hurricane had been shot down. He had managed to get out but was very badly burnt and in a serious condition. He had been some time getting to us and, although our Field Ambulance lads had done all they could, he was in a horrendous state. We got him on to the operating table, cut all his clothes off including any skin that had fused to them, then did a clean up job the best we could. Finally we wrapped him in Vaseline gauze, powdered him in sulphanilamide and put on a complete cast, virtually covering his whole body. We didn't know whether all this would work; it was a last ditch effort, there was nothing else we could do. We all thought he would probably die because of the extensive burns and our adhoc treatment. We put him on plasma drip and hoped he would make it. We kept him at the hospital because he was too ill to move, but after three weeks we put him outside in a tent by himself due to the smell and because the other patients complaining about it. Flies had laid their eggs inside the plaster and of course hundreds of maggots hatched. We knew this would happen and we hoped the maggots would get rid of all the bad and burned flesh. By this time the patient had got used to the smell, but when the maggots first came it nearly sent him mad with the constant itching; we had a hell of a game with him. Remarkably, he did improve, much to our surprise and so, we decided to cut the plaster off. We put him outside and did it in relays because the smell was so diabolical and making everybody ill. Eventually, we got the plaster off and hosed him down with water. When we finally approached him he was perfectly clean, the maggots had done their job and all the flesh and skin had grown back, but of course was red raw and acutely tender. We left him outside in the shade everyday and gradually the skin started to harden and after a week of being exposed to the elements he was able to put some clothes on. In the end, he was sent back to India and then to the UK; he was scarred, but had all his faculties. I have to say, he was a very lucky man, but exceedingly brave; the pain must have been awful, but he complained very little.

It was terribly hard to cope with the constant presence of death and horror surrounding us twenty four hours a day. You could smell and taste it. I can think of few things worse than struggling to save someone's life and just as we were finishing the operation, we lost them. I've seen the surgeon do everything to save them, even opening up the body with his scalpel and massaging the heart with his hands. It worked sometimes. In the cases where patients were lost, we would look at each other and he'd just say, "Bring in the next case". He wasn't being uncaring, far from it. It was that we were used to the hopelessness of the situation and developed a hard outer shell. We couldn't let the others see that it got to us, especially the other patients. They depended on us. We couldn't show any sign of weakness. There were medics there that twelve months previously couldn't put on a sticking plaster and now they were looking after patients at death's door

Wherever possible the dead were buried quickly because of decomposition and the flies, but at night those that didn't make it were taken to the mortuary tent and there could be quite a few in there during a busy period. It wasn't a pleasant place to say the least, rats were ever present. I recall going in one morning and seeing one exit out of some poor dead chap's cheek. On another occasion, I have seen bodies infested with maggots because of the speed of decomposition in the heat. But this was just another thing to us; we were conditioned to ignore our feelings and get on with the job in hand. It caused me a lot of anxiety after the war because I had become hard mentally and it took a long time for me to get back to normal, or as normal as you can after that.

Another case that amazed us was when a soldier just walked into the hospital came to the operating tent and said that he had got a wound in his chest. I took a look at him and told the surgeon and he said to bring him in. He explored the wound and pulled out a broken six inch bolt off the tank that had blown up with him in it. It was beyond belief that he was alive, let alone able to walk unaided for treatment. We often used to wonder how much the human body could stand and it always seemed that the fellows with the worst wounds were the last to complain. On the other hand, we had some troops in who had self-inflicted wounds. Rather than go into battle they shot themselves through the foot or hand; they were mostly Indian. We attended to them at the time, but when they were better we sent them back to their unit with a recommendation that they should be court martialled.

When we knew the 14th British General Hospital had become fully operational, we diverted lots of the aircraft full of casualties there. We needed to slow down and rest and thought we'd let them have a go. Our CO hadn't forgotten how they dropped us in it when they pulled out at Kanglatongbi. However, when a senior officer was injured up at the front, I had the job of flying there to collect him in a little Stimpson aircraft. It was ever so small and only had room for the pilot, a stretcher case and one other, me. We flew to a clearing in the jungle picked up the patient and flew him straight back to Imphal for treatment. It became a regular trip, usually for head injuries and it made a change for me, a break from routine and a chance to see places. I preferred that.

During a lull when we were awaiting more supplies, the CO, two officers and myself flew up to a landing strip at the front, which the 14th

Army had just taken from the Japs. We went to see if any of the gliders which took troops in could be used to bring the injured out, so had a trial run. They were awful things; on the take off you nearly broke your neck and then it was a hell of a bumpy ride over the mountains and the landing wasn't much to be desired; no wheels, just skids. We discussed it, but although it would have been quicker, we thought that some of the patients wouldn't make the journey. It may have done more harm than good. I don't think they bothered with the idea in the end.

In November, the surgeon Lt. Colonel, two other officers and me, boarded a DC3 aircraft and away we went. I hadn't a clue where we were going. All the Colonel had said was to get tidied up and report to his tent in twenty minutes, so I did. We all got into a jeep and went straight to the airstrip and onto a plane. It was only then that I found out that we were going to Chunking in China. We flew over the east of the Himalayas and Bhutan, a long flight over the 'hump' as they called that part of the mountain range, which incidentally was the place where General Wingate was killed. Finally, we landed, but I never really found out what it was all about. I believe our CO wanted to set up a hospital in that area. He was a mad sort and would have loved to do that, just for the experience. I asked him what he wanted me to do. He said nothing and just thought I would like the trip, which of course, I did. We went to the USA base there. We soon got friendly with them and had a great time. The Yanks were cutting roads through thick jungle and they were marvellous at it. The Chinese troops there went out on sorties against the Japs. I spent a while with them and found they were quite a happy crowd. Mind you, I wondered how they knew who was who, they and the Japs looked so alike and even wore the same sort of clothing. I remember thinking, I wouldn't fancy being in action with them. I wouldn't know who to shoot. The Americans and Chinese were a great bunch. The Yanks seemed to be real tough guys, most of them Texans and they were all huge men, well over six feet tall. I had my meals in their mess; steaks, canned beer, spirits, the lot. They really lived well; thought more of food than anything else; in the British Army it's tea. Unfortunately we had to go back and we left Chunking and flew back over the mountains once more. We reached Imphal without incident, but I had hell of a ribbing off the lads when I got back, over my ' jolly boys outing'.

Back at the hospital we were beginning to get more staff, six more medical orderlies and four sisters arrived, the sisters to take charge of the wards (tents). They couldn't believe the conditions we were working under. They had come from Delhi where everything was done 'all proper like'. At first the sisters thought they were back there, just giving orders, but it didn't work, everyone had to muck in together, they even had to do the cooking. One of the sisters was assigned to the operating theatre and we had a sixty case convoy of wounded come in. The surgeon had her assisting him with the operations and it was non-stop pandemonium. Well, the poor woman couldn't take it. She burst out crying. The CO didn't mince words. He told her to clear off or words to that effect and told me to scrub up and take over. After that he wouldn't have a sister in the theatre. It was a shame really, but we didn't have the time. People were dying. In the tented wards it was the same, chaotic as usual. In between each bed was a stretcher with someone on it. We were used to it, but the sisters weren't. They were in total despair. To help them out, six of the lads spent a day each with them showing them how to cope. You had to be practical. All patients that could walk were put outside and also as many stretchers as possible. If it was raining we covered them with ground sheets, put across the bamboo poles of the mosquito nets. This gave us room to see and treat the bed casualties. Anyone that could hobble was assigned to help in the general duties of the ward, such as helping with meals, making beds, in fact, anything that had to be done, there was no specific list of duties, everybody just had to pitch in. There were never any grumbles either, despite their own situation. The troops could see the conditions we were working in; we were permanently stretched to the limit. Some of the casualties showed aptitude in their hospital work so we hung on to them and evacuated as many of the others as possible. Of course, those that helped didn't want to go back up to the front again and we played on that too. They would do anything, all the worst jobs. It freed the experienced staff for the more important duties to be carried out. Eventually the sisters got the hang of things and once more the team spirit prevailed. It was impossible to improve the conditions at the hospital site itself. Firstly, it was never suitable and secondly it had deteriorated so much in the time we were there. The sanitation was primitive from the day it was put in, so you can imagine what it became like after thousands of troops had used the facilities. A new site was required quickly, but we were told to hang on till after Christmas.

December 25th came but nobody noticed it. There wasn't even a service. The Padre was ill. We had no booze, no fags, nothing and to cap it all a plane load of wounded came in. I worked all Christmas Day and right up to five thirty on the Boxing Day morning. Not a merry Christmas at all. We were told that the troops up at the front had the Japs on the run, but not without cost to our men in casualties, which in turn made our job very hectic indeed. We never seemed to have chance to catch up with things or make any improvements. We were just managing to cope and all were beginning to feel the strain again.

In mid January, we were told that the hospital was being moved to another site forward of Imphal, south of the airstrip. We went up to have a look and saw the bulldozers tearing up the trees and levelling the site. It was better than where we were, nothing fantastic, but a much-improved position. We didn't know how long we would stay at the new site. You never did out there. Nothing was permanent because as the front line moved forward, so did we.

Eventually, the big move started. First all the patients had to be evacuated, over two thousand of them. Most went by air, that was the worst cases, but the others went by road all the way back to bases in India. I remember thinking God help them because it was such a long and arduous trip. We never knew how they got on. It would have been interesting to find out, even fit men paled at such a journey. The Colonel said we had been given four days to move and be operational again. Originally new tents should have been erected for us to move straight into, but this was the army and things didn't work out like that. The new stuff was still somewhere in India, the usual cock up. So, we tore down our old mucky tents, put them on trucks and erected them on the new site about thirty miles away. It was a mammoth task when you consider the physical effort involved and the amount of equipment to move; about four hundred and fifty tons. The Indian labour force helped us, we wouldn't have done it otherwise. They really did work hard. They worked all day and night until the job was done. As soon as tents were pulled down they were quickly rushed to the new site and erected straight away. There was no time to waste. Beds were immediately moved in with all the equipment needed. It was very basic but functional. I erected the operating theatre with one of the other chaps and fully equipped it. All the hard work paid off and within four days we were fully operational and nearly full of patients. In fact, even on the second day we were doing operations and that was no mean feat. The CO came round thanked us all for the effort which was very nice, but we were all knackered and could have done with another stint of leave, but there was no hope of that.

The Japs had occupied the hill we were on and there were bunkers all over it. They were well built as well and it was no wonder it took our troops some time to get them out. The hospital was situated at the bottom of the hill on flat ground, with our tents on platforms cut out of the hillside. The floors were covered in thick gravel and this was dry and made a change for us. We obtained some new tents, which meant we had six in a tent instead of ten and to add to our new found luxury, we had a new cookhouse and mess tent and much better rations. It was a lot better. We had some new arrivals to help out including some more sisters. The original gang of twenty were now standing down, teaching the others what to do and getting a little more time off. Things were looking up and we hoped they would remain that way.

We were told that Noel Coward was coming to Imphal to entertain us, so a medium sized tent was put up near the hospital and airstrip. Typically, we were in the throes of the monsoon, non stop rain night and day and everywhere was swamped. A truck appeared with a piano on it. With difficulty, they managed to get the instrument off and position it fairly upright on some boards inside the tent. A stool was made out of bamboo for him to sit on and eventually the show was ready to start. The troops had to be rounded up on a 'see it or else' basis. They were all so apathetic. The point was, who wanted to watch someone singing 'Mad dogs and Englishmen go out in the midday sun' in the middle of a monsoon? Anyway, the fun started and Noel sat on the seat and commenced. Well, it was hilarious, the stool slowly sank into the mud and the piano went down at an angle and when he started to play it, it was completely out of tune. The hot, steamy, humid atmosphere had got at the wires. You can imagine the roars of laughter from the troops. They thought it was brilliant. I wouldn't have missed it for all the tea in China. But of course, Noel Coward was not amused at all. Actually, he was downright niggly about it and splashed out of the tent in a right rage, to the raucous cheers of the men. We never saw him again. However, I must say this about him, he was the only one other than Stainless Stephen that came as far as Imphal to entertain the troops and we appreciated that. He gave us one a hell of a laugh, just when we needed it.

CHAPTER SEVEN

I received a telegram from Vera, my sister on 18th January 1945. It said that my father had died on 13th December 1944. It was a terrible shock. He had died of a heart attack, complicated by bronchitis; I didn't even know he was ill. I was devastated. I had been looking forward so much to a reunion when I got home. There was so much to tell them and Dad would have understood. Now there was nothing, just a big empty space. It left Vera and myself and she was only a kid really and on her own. What would she do? I walked to the top of a hill nearby and sat for a couple of hours trying to sort things out. I was in the same state as many of my comrades who had lost wives, sweethearts, limbs, eyes, etc. and it had been my job to try and comfort them. I realised how hard it was to accept the loss. I had always had faith in myself and I was baptised a Christian and believed help would be at hand if I needed it. I said a little prayer and asked for guidance and it was answered.

I told the Colonel about my predicament and he said he would try for compassionate repatriation for me. I said I was really worried about Vera and the house and he arranged for the Army Welfare in Britain to sort it out. It was impossible for immediate repatriation because of conditions where we were and I was the only 1st class operating assistant in the area and couldn't be spared. Furthermore, it was too late to go to the funeral. Soon after an officer from the welfare side of the army came to see a number of us to try to sort out our problems back home. He said an aunt was taking care of Vera and the house was transferred to my name. Lodgers were to be put in it until I returned home. The officer said Vera had been seen by the Army Welfare and that she was well and they would check on her from time to time to make sure she was all right. That was a relief. I was really worried about her. I was also very relieved about the house, for now at least, I had somewhere to go when I got home. I didn't want to stay with relatives, I wanted my own place. All I had to do now was survive.

Owing to the break out of Imphal by the 14th Army and the continuing advance of our troops, General Slim had his caravan brought forward in which he conducted his strategy of the war. It was parked right near us and we saw quite a lot of him and also Louis Mountbatten. He used to go to different parts of the front line and address the troops and tell them what was going on, which was a good thing because we wondered what the hell was happening half the time. He also said we now had the initiative and the Japs were on the run and that there would be no let up, despite the weather and new and better equipment was to be brought into action. He certainly boosted the morale of the troops. It was needed. There had been so many empty promises in the past.

During January and February, two or three of us at a time were posted to the Chindwin area to relieve some of the Casualty Clearing Station medics who had gone down with dysentery or malaria. We knew what it was all about regarding the work, we'd already done it. It was non-stop - no change there. I also went with the CO up near the front to see about setting up a new hospital site, but the army was moving forward so fast, it would be a waste of time. It was easier to fly the men out as airfields were captured and other temporary ones built, either to our base hospital, the 41st IGH, or to Comilla, Chittagong, Dacca or Cox's Bazaar areas which were now Jap free.

My CO was always up for something new. He even had an idea of setting up a paramedics unit, to go in with the paratroops on forward missions. He got two officers, three others and me plus himself, to do two parachute jumps as a practice. We had scanty training of a couple hours, told what we were to do when we baled out and that was all we did. Then, they stuck us on a DC3 aircraft and away we went. We did the first jump on open ground, which wasn't too bad, but the second jump was near some hills and the turbulence sent us all over the place. We went one way and the equipment went somewhere else and got lost in the wilderness. The whole idea was shelved and put on some pending file, which meant that was that. I wasn't that disappointed, I wasn't really keen on the idea but it was a great thrill doing the parachuting, something really different.

The weather at this time was very wet and humid and seemed to change all the while. It was very rare to have stable conditions. It didn't really matter to us though. We had to get on with it whatever the weather.

The letter situation got slightly better and we were averaging three a month, which was good. It gave us the opportunity to know what was happening at home, which was important to me, especially with Vera and the house on my mind. It was good for morale too. The blokes were happier for it. More supplies were pouring in and a lot of mules and pack horses arrived, essential to carry the supplies up into the hills and over the rough terrain. We had a Royal Army Veterinary Corps depot next to our site and when we had time to spare we took out some of the horses they had there to keep them exercised. It was great and it made a change. I became very good at riding after a while. We had a hurricane one night and it blew three quarters of the hospital down. It was a dreadful mess. All of us worked through the night. We had no lights and there was a terrific howling wind and torrential rain. When it started to get light we could see the extent of the damage. It was hard to believe. There were rows of patients lying on their beds in the pouring rain where the tents had blown away. Others were stuck under the tents that had fallen on them. We feared the worse at first yet, when it was sorted out, very few of the patients had suffered any additional injuries.

The hospital was still working at full capacity. Aircraft were bringing in a lot of casualties and it was common practice to work all day and night. When possible I would go to my tent and have a lie down, but that could be at any time. We had no set hours of work. The lads were very good and would keep fairly quiet while I got some rest. We tried to organise things in the theatre so that we could sleep at night but it was rarely possible. I would be in the middle of a deep sleep at two o'clock in the morning and a sepoy would be shaking me up, saying the Colonel wanted me at the theatre. You couldn't refuse. That wasn't my style. So, I would quickly get dressed, grab my tiny oil lamp and walk down the tiny narrow paths to the theatre. They were quite eerie, pitch black, always raining and with the continuous, foreboding noise of the jungle. There were also huge frogs and snakes about. They were fairly safe though, as long as you didn't tread on them. You had to be careful.

The CO managed to acquire a diesel run electric generator, just for lights and we managed to get two electric lights in each tent (ward). The REME flattened some corned beef tins and made us a four-bulb light for the operating theatre. It made a tremendous difference and was put above the operating table. This was a real luxury for us and was very useful when you consider we used to do major operations just with the light from the oil lamps. The down side to all this was the generator took four of us to start it, by handle. There was no starter motor and it was very noisy, but we could live with that. The advantages far outweighed the disadvantages.

We had a bad do one night. A huge ammunition dump blew up. They thought it was the work of the Japanese raised Indian National Army (Jiffs), a group of mixed races, mostly Indian, who didn't like the British and they were employed by the Japs to do sabotage. They were quite dangerous and could mix in unnoticed amongst the Indian troops and wore the same uniform. The ammunition was stored in tunnels cut out of the inside of a hill and when it went up, it blew the top right off. Apparently, they stored all sorts there and it went off with a tremendous force; bombs, shells, boxes of bullets. Our hospital was less than half a mile away and with our tents being on the perimeter of the site, we could feel the blast, so we all lay on the floor. There was loads of debris flying about, so we had to be careful. After a while it quietened down. Most of the big bombs had gone off, but there was still plenty of the smaller stuff banging away. I had a message to go to the theatre and met Colonel D'Abreu who was standing in for my CO who was ill. Colonel D'Abreu was a good surgeon and after the war became a Professor of Surgery at the Queen Elizabeth Hospital, Birmingham. He told me to prepare for spleen operations, there were bound to be some caused by the blast and also for general wounds. As usual all the instruments went into the sterilisers and we waited and then they came. The first six cases all had ruptured spleens but to make matters worse, all the helpers that should have been in the theatre to aid us had been sent down to help at the blast site. There were very few other cases, as it appeared that anyone in the area of the blast was killed outright. We had no alternative than to carry on and that was what we did. With just the surgeon, anaesthetist, and myself, we did the six operations on our own. We started at ten thirty in the evening and finished at six thirty the next morning.

Right at the beginning of March, three operating room assistants arrived from England, with a further twenty sisters and some more nursing orderlies. They moaned like hell about the conditions, the food, the rain, everything. I'm sure they thought we'd put the mud there on purpose. They weren't used to it you see. It was much better than it was, but we couldn't convince them of that.

We were on the move again, some of my pals and myself went forward to Shwebo, not far from Mandalay. We travelled back through Tiddim, Palel and Tamu, places where we were evacuated from, nearly two years previously. We crossed the Chindwin River and the land here was a lot flatter. It was the sort of land that we liked to fight on, you could see who's who there, not like the jungle. That was the Japs preferred battleground. They were experts in there. Our tanks, artillery and the infantry were playing hell with the enemy and the front line was always on the move. We would set up a casualty post one day and move it the next. We didn't like it, but it was in the best direction, so we couldn't complain. At last things were getting organised. All casualties were patched up and flown out the same day, either to our own hospital in Imphal or one of the others now available.

Late in March, after days of terrific bombardment, Mandalay was captured, the Japs pulled out to the south during the night and our troops more or less walked in clearing up pockets of resistance. It was a fantastic sight to see the final battle for Mandalay. We were less than half a mile away and the ground trembled. The RAF and some of the Yanks did round the clock bombing. It was a tremendous sight and certainly weakened the Japs resistance. A lot of Japs were now giving themselves up, they'd had enough. This was most unusual to us as we were led to believe that they were trained to die rather than surrender. They had taken a real pounding during the battles. A lot of dead were left lying about. The British dead were looked after by the Pioneer Corps and where possible, were buried in cemeteries. However, hundreds of Japs were left lying around, until they could be gathered together and then they were cremated. This had to be done to prevent the spread of disease. Search parties would go out and look up in the sky to see where the vultures were most active and usually there was a body there. We had the best-fed vultures in Asia. Also the flies gave an indication as to where a body would be found. There would be millions of them around it and you could hear the noise half a mile away. The rats were always very active too. One of the reasons the Japs were defeated was because of their very scanty medical services and the long lines of supply routes. They were dying from cerebral malaria, the worst type, other tropical diseases and also malnutrition. During their retreat thousands of bodies were found. Their losses must have been enormous. General Slim gave orders not to let up on the advance and the 14th Army didn't stop at Mandalay. There were no celebrations. He wanted Rangoon taken quickly and didn't want to leave the Japs any time to consolidate their forces as they still had plenty of troops left in Burma and Thailand and we had a long way to go yet. If we could get Rangoon quickly, it would mean our supply ships could dock there and we could dispense with the terrific land journey by road and rail from India. It would also give the Air Force more time for bombing rather than being used for supply drops. It looked as though it was the end of the Japs in Burma the way things were going and that was a good job. We had done our bit and it meant my repatriation would come sooner.

A lot of fresh troops arrived, some from the Middle East and they didn't like it one little bit. They were used to wide-open spaces and dry heat, but here, it was a moist heat, very overpowering and oppressive, hot and always raining, and that plus the glorious mud was a big shock. A lot of friendly banter took place between us. They would say they had come to show us how to win a war and we would ask why they took so long, considering the war in Africa finished in 1943. They got some right stick, but it was in good taste and humour and helped keep up morale.

Most of our crowd was due for repatriation. We had done more than our share now and were looking forward to going home. We'd had enough. We all fancied a newspaper full of fish and chips and a nice cold pint of British beer. We were having more help and managing to get more time off. We went to Mandalay to have a look round. I was impressed and surprised to see a lot of the pagodas had not been damaged too much, considering the terrific bombardment the airforce had given it.

On April 27th 1945, my repatriation papers came through. Three of us had the lucky break and we were told we had to get ready to move by April 30th. We had a load of casualties in just before and so we worked for forty-eight hours non-stop; quite a send off. The three of us went round saying our farewells to everyone and it seemed very strange our gang splitting up, a bit emotional really. The others should be in the next batch and even the CO would be going. We had hoped we would have all gone at the same time but the Army does not work like that and we weren't going to turn the opportunity down. Three days later we managed to get a lift on a DC3 to Imphal, which saved us a rough two-day track journey to 51st rest camp at Manipur. The next morning we got on a truck that was going to Dimapur and went through our old hospital site at Kangletombi, where the Japs had put their roadblock. We had a quick look round, but it was all desolate and overgrown now. The jungle soon took over again. Then, we made our way to Kohima had a good look round there. It was still in a hell of a mess after the epic battle that had taken place there. We had a look at the cemetery that was being built. It was tragic to see so many crosses. We had a meal and a mug of tea at the rest camp, then went to Dimapur, arriving at two o'clock the next morning. It wasn't a pleasant journey through the mountains in the dark. It left a lot to be desired, especially with the Indian drivers. They had a habit of falling asleep at the wheel. We booked into No. 5 rest camp, had a wash and clean up, plus some tea and food. We stayed at the rest camp all that day and left the next, boarded the train to Pandu, which we reached round about midday, Friday 4th May, crossed the Brahmaputra River by ferry and by train to Parbatipur. We went to an American run food centre, set up by the army for all forces going in our out of Burma and I must say it was very good, the best meal I had in months. Typically, the USA army catering service ran it and we knew they liked their food. We didn't stay long and by three o'clock, we were on another train to Calcutta, arriving on Sunday evening, reporting to the rest camp, after a weeklong journey. We seemed to spend forever on these trains, but it was the only way. Travelling by road didn't bear thinking about and there was no chance of flying out. We spent three days in Calcutta, had a good look round and sorted ourselves out, knowing we would probably never see this place again. It is too much to explain about Calcutta. It is one of those places you have to see to believe; anything and everything went on there. We were in barracks for three days and because of the stealing that went on, all the windows had steel bars on them. So what the Indians did was to find very thin lads, cover them with grease and they would squeeze between the bars at night and pinch anything they could put their hands on and pass it to the others outside. I lost a khaki jacket with all the names and addresses of my mates back in Imphal. That upset me. It was in a notebook in the pocket. My money was in a body belt, so that was safe, but some of the lads lost everything. I managed to get another jacket from the stores; told the quartermaster that's all I had to wear. It wasn't but I wasn't going to do without, especially in the circumstances.

From Calcutta we caught a train to Deolali, travelling for nearly two days solid, right across India, East to West, a hell of a trip. Deolali was a holding Depot, which dealt with repatriation of all members of the British Forces. You stayed there until a ship was available and there were sufficient men to go on it. They made sure the ships were full. Some troops stayed there quite a time waiting to be repatriated. It drove them almost crazy being so close but so far from home. They called it the

'Deolali Tap'. Incidentally, that's where the word 'doolally' comes from when you refer to someone being mad. We were seven days there and it wasn't a very nice place. As usual we were under canvas and it was very hot. We were issued with new kit, serge uniform and greatcoats for when we reached England. It was strange lugging a greatcoat around in such heat, but I suppose it was a taste of things to come. We could have done with some cooler weather anyway, it would have made a welcome change. As a matter of interest I had very little in the way of kit. My steel helmet and respirator went four years ago and I lost the rest of my kit when the Japs cut the road at Imphal. I liked the idea of travelling light, but now we were being issued with everything again, two kit bags, steel helmet, respirator and full backpack, side packs, the lot. It was really mad. We were gong home, but now I think it was a way of getting stores back to England. I was determined not to be too overburdened and decided to lose some somewhere. I hadn't signed for it in my name.

Each morning we would go to the Company office and see if our names were on the list for Movement Control to Bombay and at last, our names came up, the three of us together. This was most unusual because this was one place were you generally got separated from your pals; usually allocated to different ships. It was probably something to do with me. The Sergeant and the Corporal in the Company Office had both got venereal disease and I managed to get them some MB693 tablets that sorted them out. So the favour was returned. We left Deolali by train, early morning on the 18th May and reached Bombay in the evening and boarded the troopship Orion. It was a typical troopship in every way, overcrowded as usual, but no one cared. We were going home. We were supposed to sleep in the holds in hammocks but it was too hot and dangerous. We'd been there before, so we staked a claim to three imaginary places on the deck and these were more or less ours for the rest of the journey home; a sort of gentleman's agreement. The only problem with sleeping on deck was that every morning, about five thirty, the ships crew came round with dirty great hose pipes to wash the decks down and if you weren't sharp to move you were nearly washed over the side. We used to call them everything, but it didn't make any difference, they couldn't understand a word of English. Mind you, the decks would dry in minutes, so it was heads down again.

On May 19th 1945, we sailed out of Bombay harbour watching a hotel building called the Gateway of India slowly disappear from view. It was the last thing you saw from a distance and then just sea. I think every

The Orion - the ship on which we came home

soldier on board must have stood and watched and then gave an almighty cheer. I had mixed feelings myself. I had got used to travelling and to the open spaces and wondered whether I could face up to humdrum life at home in England. It was nice to think about going home, but to what? Vera I know, but what else? I was quite worried about it, which was strange after what I had been through, but I decided to wait and see and take one day at a time. I didn't have much choice, but that was better than one of my mates with me. He had nothing to go home to. He had survived, but his mother, father and sister were all killed in an air raid and the house had disappeared. He didn't know what to do. He said he might join the regular army. The army was all he had left.

We had a good look round the ship, found out where things were, like food and drink, the latter being tea or lime juice. There was no booze on the troopships. The food was good but conditions were far from comfortable but so what, we were used to it over the years. The war in Europe finished on 8th May 1945 and therefore, the ships were allowed to light up again after dark, which was really good. It made a nice change to the continuous darkness we had to suffer on the way out. Life on board was good, we lounged about the deck all day, lapping up the sunshine and all the troops looked happy. Life was certainly more pleasant. Except for lifeboat drill, we did nothing in the way of duties. It was almost like a holiday cruise, lying about on the decks all day in just a pair of shorts. It was very hot with virtually no breeze. We all looked a very brown mahogany colour; different to the yellow colour we had been when we boarded the ship. Discipline was kept to a minimum. In any case the troops on board behaved well considering the mixed bag on the ship. A lot of good-natured banter took place, but it was all very civil. There was no real trouble. We sailed along and eventually reached the Persian Gulf and at Bahrain, we stopped for a day to drop off some Arab troops that had come from there who, like us, were going back home. The Persian Gulf was as flat as glass, hardly a ripple on the water for miles. The only movement was the wake of the ship caused by the propellers. It was fantastic to see huge lumps of phosphorous come to the surface glowing brightly. The heat was terrific, dry, stifling, with no breeze, really hot. We sailed along and then reached Aden, situated at the entrance to the Red Sea. All ships had to anchor out in the Bay and stay there until they got permission to sail up the Red Sea and into the Suez Canal which had recently been reopened. Some ships had been sunk in it during the War in the Middle East and had to be cleared. This had been one of the reasons why we had to go round Africa on the way to India, plus it was dangerous to sail through the Mediterranean at that time. The journey through the canal was very interesting. The ships were pulled through from the port at Suez by electric power units called mules, which ran on rails each side of the canal. Propeller movement was not allowed because the wake would damage the sides of the canal. The view from the ship was not very interesting, sand dunes as far as the eye could see, except for isolated villages here and there and, of course, it was very hot. The journey through the canal was very slow but eventually we reached Port Said.

While the ship was being refuelled and restocked we were allowed ashore, three days in all. This gave us the chance to get our land legs back and have a look around the place and what a place it was. It was truly an international port, a real experience. Half the city was out of bounds because of the unsavoury antics of the Arabs and prostitution, but being British troops and full of curiosity we managed to get round quite a lot and had a lot of harmless fun and laughs. Some of us managed to get on a trip to Cairo and spent a day there and had a great time. It was a bit of a rush, but we had a good look round, a meal and a few drinks and then back to the ship by midnight. On the way back from Cairo we came back along the desert road and in the distance we could see ships going down the canal but we couldn't see the water. That was really weird, it looked as though the ships were going across the sand. Our three days in port were really crammed with sightseeing, but unfortunately, we weren't able to buy much because we couldn't draw much money from the ship. It was done on purpose to stop the troops going on a binge and causing trouble.

From Port Said we sailed on. We never knew to where, except that we would finally reach England. Our next port of call was Cyprus and again we dropped some troops ashore and were allowed one day ashore. There wasn't much time but it's surprising how much sightseeing you can get in. We all enjoyed it. It was the same when we stopped at Malta and Sicily, just a day there in each, the usual scramble, trying to put a quart into a pint pot, but we made the most of it. The ship then sailed along hugging the North African coastline, which was very good as the crew pointed out lots of places of interest. We all knew there was only one more stop before reaching home and that was Gibraltar and after two days there it was on to England, across the Bay of Biscay. As we approached England it started to get much colder. We stood it as long as we could but in the end, we had to put on our serge uniforms. That was really uncomfortable, thick and itchy, horrible. The last time I wore serge was on the way out to Freetown. It felt strange after such a long time. We had travelled all the way from Bombay in just a pair of shorts and the only time we wore a shirt was when we went ashore. I had a hell of a tan though. You couldn't buy that out of a bottle. After a bouncy journey across the Bay of Biscay, early in the morning, someone shouted "land ahead". Immediately, there was a rush up to the decks and there it was, Lands End. A big cheer went all round the ship. We docked at Liverpool on June 16th 1945, a journey of thirty-two days.

We left the boat early next morning and got on a special train to Aldershot where we checked in and were issued with some pay and ration tickets. We were given rail tickets and then sent on our way home. It was all very efficient, very strange, but typical of the army, they didn't give you time to think about anything. I was granted thirty days overseas leave and was off. I arrived at New Street Station, Birmingham but couldn't get a taxi, so I ambled across to a bus stop, which was quite near. Several people I knew from Weoley Castle went past and I had a quick word. After waiting ages I asked a chap about the times of the buses and he said the bus stop had been moved around the corner. I wasn't a pretty sight and must have looked like a fugitive from Devils Island. I was still wearing my jungle green outfit and slouch hat (Aussie type), long hair and a beard. Anyway, I went to the bus stop around the corner and waited there. I caused chaos getting on the bus; two kit bags, full back pack and side packs. It was a good job I had dumped the respirator and steel helmet somewhere in the Indian Ocean. I wouldn't have been able to get on the bus at all. It was full as it was. The conductor was all right about it all. When I reached home, he stopped the bus right at the gate.

There I was home. It was nine thirty in the evening when I got there. I knocked on the door but no one was in. It was too late to go to my aunt's house, which was quite a distance away in Quinton. I was pondering what to do, when Mr Morgan who lived opposite and was a friend of my Dad said I could sleep there for the night, which I did, with thanks. I thought afterwards, why I didn't go to my aunt's in the first place, but I just wanted to see home.

The next morning I went to where my sister Vera worked and when she saw me she fell to bits. She knew I was on my way home from Burma, but didn't know when and I had no way of telling her. Things had happened so fast from when we disembarked at Liverpool. I did send a telegram but she didn't get it. She had no idea when I would get there. She just put her coat on and walked out of the shop and said to the Manager, "I'll see you sometime". When I left she was only thirteen years of age and a bit gawky and spindly as they are at that age, but she was seventeen when I returned and the difference was fantastic. She was beautiful, quite a debutante. We went down to our home, had a look in, spoke to the lodgers for a short while, picked up my kit from the Morgans and then made our way up to my aunt's house, where Vera had been staying since Dad died. I also stayed my leave there. It would have been impossible to stay at my own house. It was a real mess, so I left the lodgers in peace. I would wait until I was demobbed and sort it out then.

Everybody was pleased to see me and offered their condolences about Dad. But to me, I was still miles away. He was that missing link that would have made all the difference. I spent a lot of my leave trying to tie up the loose ends, meeting people, trying to trace some of my old mates and generally trying to get the feel of things. Vera took a week off so we went around quite a bit, seeing what had happened over the years I had been away. The bombing had certainly knocked Birmingham about. It was all very different especially after all that time.

I found people were very good to me everywhere I went, a pub, cafe, tea bar, I rarely had to pay. They wouldn't take any money off me. It appears I was in the first batch of troops to come from Burma and few people had seen the jungle green outfit. It created quite a stir. During my leave I went to see some of the parents of some of my mates who were still in Burma and told them they were okay and were waiting to come home, which would be soon. They were very pleased and appreciated my visits, shed a few tears, but were very relieved. The worst thing that affected me and I couldn't get used to it, was sleeping in a small room. It felt like being in a cell. I felt the walls would collapse in. It was the same walking down a street or in town. You see, I had been so used to open spaces, nothing for miles, lots of room. It was very depressing being so closed in. I have spoken to other fellows about it and they said they felt the same. Of course, there was no counselling then, you had to get on with it. I did.

The thirty days leave soon went by and I returned on Saturday July 14th. I had to report to Boyce Barracks in Aldershot. We slept on beds there and that made a change from the floor. I had my kit made up again. I had left most of the good stuff at home on purpose. I said I had joined the ship on the last minute and had no time to re-kit at Deolali. No-one questioned it. Then, I went for an interview with the CO. He wanted me to stay in Aldershot to train the new recruits. He said he would make me a staff sergeant immediately, but I came up with the case that I would like to be near home because of domestic circumstances and Vera being young and on her own. It went down well with him, but in fact, I didn't want to stop there; too much bull and regimentation. I wasn't used to it now and Aldershot was a right dump and full of Red Caps. Then he said would Shrewsbury suit me and I accepted, not too enthusiastically in case he changed his mind. By the next Tuesday I was on my way to Shrewsbury. On Wednesday I had an interview with the Colonel in charge. He told me he was an ex Burma Wallah in the Chittagong area, but he knew of Imphal and what had taken place there. I couldn't go wrong. I told him I didn't want to go back to the operating theatre work, I'd had enough of that. The truth was it was too tying, you were always on call and I wanted more freedom. Also it took me months to get the constant smell of blood and death out of my system. I told him all this and he understood. He asked me what I did in civvy life and I said I worked in the retail grocery trade. He was pleased about this and put me in charge of the Ration Stores. Apparently, there was a lot of trouble going on there. Lots of rations were going missing and he was scared the auditors would move in. I think he was involved in it, but he didn't say so. I said I would do it and get it straight but wouldn't sign for the stores until I had sorted it out. He agreed, he had no need to, he could have ordered me to do so. Within a month I had by devious means got the rations into credit and that's a story on its own. The Army Auditors came and went right through the books and the stores but everything was all right. The Colonel sent for me and he was really pleased and then informed me that I was to take over all the clothing and ration stores in the hospital. I didn't mind though.

One of my duties was to go round the civvy hospitals and institutions that had taken in some of the troops and arrange for them to have civvy clothes before they were discharged from the forces. Unfortunately, some of them would never see outside hospitals again. They were in a terrible state, dying of tuberculosis and other diseases. Others had horrific injuries and quite a lot were blind. It was very upsetting to see them. You felt so helpless. You wished you could do something for them. We used to cheer them up the best we could, try and get a laugh out of them, but they knew. The sad thing is that some are still in care today.

Then the Japs surrendered on August 14th 1945. Now that the hostilities had ended, came the demobilisation. It was a massive task and it fell on us to arrange demob for a lot of troops and patients and also, some prisoners of war, mainly Italians and a few Germans. All troops going on demob had to hand in their equipment; all that they were allowed to take was one uniform, shirt, vest, pants, socks and a pair of boots. Anything missing from the kit that was handed in was deducted from their final pay. It fell on my Clothing Stores to 'de-kit' hundreds of troops. I had about twenty chaps working for me and they were hard to motivate. They were all waiting for demob, same as me and couldn't care less. We just kept our noses clean as the phrase goes.

My life in Shrewsbury was great, such a change to what I had been used to abroad. What really made the change was meeting up with a girl called Mabel after a month there. We went out on a regular basis and I was really made welcome by her family. It was only then that I felt I had reached home. Life began to take on a new meaning. It had been quite empty before. I couldn't see any end product. Mabel and I had a great time together and saw each other as much as possible, in between our duties. Anyway Mabel and I were waiting for my demob to come through before we decided to get married and settle down in Weoley Castle. Mabel was no stranger to Birmingham. She had been drafted there during the war, working on Spitfires and Lancaster Bombers.

I knew my demob number was coming up in June sometime but in May I was sent for to see the CO. He said that since I was the only operating room assistant class one in the area and being a Corporal, GHQ he had decided to post me to a hospital ship that was going round the world. It was taking severely injured patients home to their various countries and it would be a six-month posting. I didn't fancy that at all and told the CO that since I was getting married and sorting the house out, couldn't he get somebody else. He said no, I had to go. I was devastated. But he didn't bank on my mates at the Company Office. They drafted a chap in from another area. They wangled his papers and made him an operating assistant class one and made up his rank to a Corporal. The CO didn't know. He had left the unit to go elsewhere, so it let me off the hook. I had travelled enough and of course, the main reason was that I didn't want to leave Mabel.

I was released from the Army on June 16th 1946, went to Bradford to be fitted with civvy clothes; that was a suit, raincoat, shirt, hat and shoes. Then I went to my aunt's house pending taking over at my own home. The lodgers had been found other accommodation and the house was empty. While Mabel was in Shrewsbury preparing for the wedding, I slept at my aunt's at night but during the day was trying to get things in order at home. It was a real mess. The lodgers hadn't bothered to do much. They knew they were leaving. What made things more difficult was the fact that materials were hard to get, wallpaper was virtually impossible to obtain, so all the walls had to be walloped with a kind of emulsion but not as good; rub against it and it would be all over your clothes. Back at home I had been taking stock of things. It didn't take long; it had all gone. When I went into the Army we had most things at home, but now it was derelict. I don't know what happened to it, except that it wasn't there. All my clothes had gone, so had all the bed linen, everything of any use, but so what, I wasn't bothered. It didn't matter, it was one of those things. I had a new life ahead of me now. I remembered saying to Dad before I left that he could use any of my clothes he wanted. I couldn't see them fitting me when I got back. He took me at my word; he wore the lot, shirts, trousers, vests, pants, everything. There was nothing left. Fair play to him, he said he would and he did. The ironic thing was that when I returned I was exactly the same size as when I went out.

Rationing was still very tight and clothing was on coupons, so it was an awkward time for anyone to get married, but we were determined to see it through. We even had to get special permission; something to do with the army, but Mabel sorted it out as usual. Mabel and I married a month later, on St Swithun's Day. Our wedding day came along quickly.

My best man was Bill Aspry. He had recently arrived home from Burma, where we had worked together in the 41st Indian General Hospital. Tom, my cousin who was in the Coldstream Guards was also there and of course, Vera. We married at Bicton Church, just outside Shrewsbury, a lovely old village church and had a wonderful service and reception. Everything went great, thanks to Mabel who had arranged it all. In the evening we went to Birmingham by train and arrived at our new home just after midnight.

I took all my leave due to me. It finished on August 11th and then the nasty bit, I had to go back to work. The Government had passed a law when we were called up, that the jobs we were in had to be available when, or if, we returned from the war. It was good really because jobs were hard to get. But the change over from war to peace left things flat. Nothing seemed to be organised. Everything was in a muddle; it was nobody's fault. It was just one of those things. Rationing was very tight, in fact, worse than it had been. You needed coupons for clothing and had to get a special docket to get some bedclothes and furniture, but we got by. I returned to Wrensons at Weoley Castle, taking up my old job. I could have gone into the hospital as an operating assistant, but the pay was no good, only ⟨3⟩ pound ten shillings per week (£3.50) and I was earning over four pounds where I was. I realised it was a waste of a trade or talent, but I had just got married and needed the money. That was more important to me. I found it hard to re-adjust. I was lucky, some poor chaps couldn't. There was no treatment or compensation for war trauma then. They left you to it. People didn't understand, I was so used to a different lifestyle. It's difficult to describe, but the war was like an adventure and I missed it. There was no satisfaction in being stuck in a poky little shop, serving someone half a pound of carrots across the counter. I was restless and wanted to see and feel the open spaces again, but I knew I wouldn't. With Mabel's help I settled down as best I could and got on with it. I stayed in the retail trade all my working life, eventually managing a large supermarket for one of the large chain-stores, so it didn't turn out too badly. Vera married sometime after and moved to Italy to live, returning back home some years later. I often see her. Mabel and I have two children, a boy and a girl, just right. They have children of their own now and it's lovely when they visit us here, still at the same house, in Gregory Avenue. So as you can see, I did get on with it and settled down quite well in the end...but I still miss it!